Survey of American Poetry

Volume VIII
Interval Between World Wars
1920-1939

Poetry Anthology Press

The World's Best Poetry

Survey of American Poetry

Survey of American Poetry

Volume VIII
Interval Between World Wars
1920-1939

Prepared by
The Editorial Board, Roth Publishing, Inc.
(formerly Granger Book Co., Inc.)

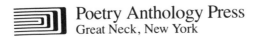 Poetry Anthology Press
Great Neck, New York

Copyright © Roth Publishing, Inc. 1986
All rights reserved

Library of Congress Catalog Card Number 81-83526
International Standard Book Number 0-89609-220-8
International Standard Book Number for
Foundation Volumes I-X, 0-89609-299-2

Manufactured in the U.S.A.

Poetry Anthology Press is a
division of Roth Publishing, Inc.
(formerly Granger Book Co., Inc.)

CONTENTS

Preface

The publications of **Poetry Anthology Press** constitute a comprehensive conspectus of international verse in English designed to form the core of a library's poetry collection. Covering the entire range of poetic literature, these anthologies encompass all topics and national literatures.

Each collection, published in a multivolume continuing series format, is devoted to a major area of the whole undertaking and contains complete author, title, and first line indexes. Biographical data is also provided.

The World's Best Poetry, with coverage through the 19th century, is topically classified and arranged by subject matter. Supplements keep the 10 volume foundation collection current and complete.

Survey of American Poetry is an anthology of American verse arranged chronologically in 10 volumes. Each volume presents a significant period of American poetic history, from 1607 to date.

INTRODUCTION

The period between World War I and World War II marks a continuing phase in the revival of American poetry, which began ten years prior with the birth of the modernist movement. The changes espoused by the early modernists were initially viewed as quite radical; however, by the present period, they were accepted as the norm by most poets. The modernists continued to innovate and influence poetry throughout the twenties and thirties, but reshaping the character of modern verse was no longer their only concern. The years between World Wars was a trying time in U.S. and world history, and the events during this time occasioned a range of responses among poets. T.S. Eliot felt that the very foundations of Western society were crumbling; Southern poets, such as John Crowe Ransom, sought to turn the clock back to simpler times; Black poets, such as Langston Hughes, bristled at the injustices their people were forced to endure; Archibald MacLeish rallied for poets to involve themselves in the momentous political issues of the times. In order to gain insight into these varied reactions, it is important to understand the historical context in which the poets were writing.

The election of 1920 was perceived largely as a referendum on the Treaty of Versailles, the League of Nations, and the idealism that had characterized President Woodrow Wilson's approach to foreign policy. Failing health had put an end to Wilson's political life, and, in his stead, the Democrats nominated the governor of Ohio, James M. Cox. After a great deal of internal squabbling, the Republicans chose Warren G. Harding, a senator from Ohio. The race was not even close; Harding decisively won the popular vote and out-tallied Cox in electoral votes 404 to 127. The war had cost the United States dearly in terms of human and material resources; as such, Americans had little sympathy for internationalist sentiment. They simply wished to resume their lives and return to normalcy. The rhetoric that had styled World War I to be "the war to end all wars" was largely forgotten, and, after a brief post-war depression, the country settled into a period of real prosperity. Under Harding, the cause of social reform fell dormant, as the Republicans held to their traditional stance that the best way to help the general populace was to help business.

Harding's administration, though brief (he died suddenly in 1923), was darkened by numerous scandals, such as the conviction of the Secretary of the Interior, Albert Fall, for bribery, and the dismissal of the Attorney General for a variety of improprieties, including the selling of liquor licenses and pardons. Upon Harding's death, Calvin Coolidge became President and was elected in his own right the following year. He has been criticized as being a "do-nothing" President (his laissez-faire philosophy called for leaving business unshackled), but, during the prosperous twenties, his conservative policies were attractive to many. Governmental regulations of business were relaxed, the courts repeatedly ruled against labor organizations, mergers flourished as antitrust laws were overlooked, and tariffs were raised. Yet, if government was scaled to the interests of big business and the wealthy few, it still remained that the standard of living did improve during these years for a majority of Americans.

Along with this boost in the economy, various technologies were also flourishing. Henry Ford revolutionized the production process with the assembly line, and cars were made affordable to a large segment of the public. Of course, the popularity of the automobile resulted in a great demand for gasoline, and the petroleum industry experienced a commensurate boom, as did the steel and rubber industries. Aviation also came into its own during these years. The technology had been perfected during the war, and, after Lindberg's solo crossing of the Atlantic in 1927, the airplane became an increasingly important means of transportation. Regarding the mass media, it was in the twenties that radio and motion pictures became widely available. The radio helped stimulate markets for new products, and "talkies" became commonplace by the end of the decade.

Although Coolidge, doubtlessly, could have won again in the 1928 election, he decided to step down. In his place, the Republicans nominated Herbert Hoover, who resoundingly defeated Al Smith, the Catholic governor of New York. Upon his inauguration in the spring of 1929, Hoover expressed great optimism regarding the nation's economy; yet, by the fall of that year, the economy had utterly collapsed, and the country was mired in what came to be known as the Great Depression. The situation would not take a turn for the better until a new President had taken office, and the balance of power in America had been shifted from the Republicans to the Democrats. Certainly, Hoover cannot bear full responsibility for the Great Depression; his administration fell victim to the ill-conceived policies of those who came before him. However, Hoover did fail to deal promptly and effectively with the grievous problems that faced him. He mistakenly believed that the depression would soon end and that better times would shortly follow. He also exacerbated troubles by signing the Hawley-Smoot bill into law, which raised tariffs to their highest level ever and set off a chain reaction that crippled international trade. Additional causes of the Depression included the overexpansion of agriculture and industry, overspeculation, and widescale unemployment that resulted from breakthroughs in automation. Wealth was increasingly concentrated in the hands of the few, and, thus, with so many poor and unemployed consumers, the market for manufactured goods dried up.

In the 1930 election, the Democrats took control of Congress, and, in the Presidential election two years later, their candidate, Franklin Delano Roosevelt, won a victory of landslide proportions. Roosevelt called his plan for addressing the nation's ills "the New Deal." First and foremost, the New Deal provided for the formation of various agencies to supply food and shelter for those out of work. However, as opposed to a strict dole system, these agencies (such as the Civil Works Administration and the Works Progress Administration) required that citizens work for their remuneration. Roosevelt moved swiftly and decisively to implement desperately needed reform in such areas as the monetary system, banking, agriculture, housing, and labor rights. Perhaps the most far-reaching of Roosevelt's many reforms was the passing of the Social Security Act in 1935. This law provided retirement benefits for those 65 and over, assistance to disabled persons, and unemployment benefits as well.

Tensions that would lead to the Second World War were growing when Roosevelt was elected to a second term in 1936. In 1933, Adolf Hitler had come to power in Germany amd made clear his intention to overthrow the Treaty of Versailles and restore Germany to a position of power. He withdrew his country from the League of Nations and, in 1936, openly defied the League by retaking the Rhineland. In 1938, he annexed Austria, and, in March of 1939, he overtook most of Czechoslovakia. World War II broke out on September 1, 1939, when the Germans launched their "blitzkrieg" invasion of Poland.

Americans, however, were still hurting from World War I and were anxious not to entangle themselves in another European conflict. As early as 1934, the Nye Committee helped to encourage isolationism by its investigation of the munitions industry. Munitions makers had profited enormously from the previous war, and the Committee hinted that arms manufacturers had led the U.S. into the first global conflict. In the same year, the Johnson Act forbade governments who had defaulted on debts from World War I to raise loans in the U.S. Thus, among European nations, only Finland was able to finance its war against Hitler in this manner. Finally, a series of neutrality acts were passed by Congress (1936-38) that further curtailed U.S. participation in the Allies' cause. Of course, despite all efforts to the contrary, America could not escape involvement, and, on December 8, 1941, after Japan's bombing of Pearl Harbor, the United States was once again at war.

The two World Wars frame one of the richest and most interesting periods of American verse. During these years, the "new poetry" that had begun to take shape in the second decade of the nineteenth century gained wider and wider acceptance among the public, as well as among upcoming writers. The changes that early modernist innovators such as Ezra Pound, Amy Lowell, and William Carlos Williams fought for–free verse, concision, idiomatic language, unrestricted subject matter–had by now all but eclipsed the traditional, often sentimental approach to verse that had held sway in America at the turn of the century. Certainly, people continued to write conventional verse, but, among serious writers, the new poetics had firmly established itself. The institutionalization of the "new poetry" came about in two main ways: first, the proliferation of "little magazines" during these formative years offered both a forum for experimental verse and an outlet for the seemingly countless critical essays and manifestos that gave definition to the movement. Some of the important journals of the time include *Blast* (1914-15, in London), *The Seven Arts* (1916-17, in New York), *The Dial* (1880-1929, in New York), *The Fugitive* (1922-25, in Memphis), and T.S. Eliot's *The Criterion* (1922-39). Second, after the First World War, it became increasingly common to find leading writers on college faculties; thus, an acceptance of modernism was thereby fostered in academic circles and among young readers.

The prototypical–and classic–poem of the modernist era is *The Waste Land*, by T.S. Eliot, which was published in 1922. In sharp contrast to the romantic ideal of nature, the poem is set in the city and presents a vivid, realistic picture of the modern urban experience; Eliot was unafraid to render all of the sordid aspects. Perhaps these bleak scenarios were not new to the novel (one need only think of Dickens), but they had been largely glossed over in verse. Structurally, *The Waste Land* is divided into five sections of varying lengths and is composed in a variety of verse forms. There is no coherent narrative voice to the poem but rather a series of different voices and perspectives. Indeed, *The Waste Land* is made up of apparently disparate fragments which are related to one another by some unconscious, dreamlike train of associations. (The writings of Sigmund Freud on the processes of the human unconscious were very much in the intellectual–and even popular–fore at this time.) Symbols, images, scenes, and snippets of conversations recur or are juxtaposed. The poem is charged with echoes of past literatures: Dante's *Inferno*, Elizabethan drama, The Bible, classical mythology, sacred Hindu texts–even rowdy soldier's ballads. Some compared this technique to montage in film, cubism in art, or the use of leitmotifs in music. The fascinating thing about Eliot's poem is that while in tone and outlook it seems so brutally severed from the past, its constant appropriation of materials from past cultures reveals a deep, abiding concern with tradition. In this, as much as in its fragmentation, formal inventiveness, and subject matter, *The Waste Land* epitomizes the most prevalent aims of modernist writing, which sought to incorporate the best of the past into new creative projects. One can argue that this process of appropriation had a concrete counterpart in the expatriation of many American artists of this time. Their exodus involved not simply the rejection of the crass, materialistic values of their capitalistic homeland, but a search throughout all cultures (European, Eastern, American) for those traditions that were most worthy and useful.

A group of Southern poets and critics called the Fugitives were similarly disenchanted with American society but reacted in a different manner. They attributed their country's ills to the moral, intellectual, and aesthetic sensibility fostered in the citified, industrialized North. The Fugitives called for an agrarian economy and a return to the simpler, clearer values of the South: close ties with family and community, traditional Protestant religious values, and the calming atmosphere of a rural environment. Though they were careful to repudiate the myth of the old plantation South, they yearned for a well-defined social structure. Figures such as John Crowe Ransom, Allen Tate, Donald Davidson, Robert Penn Warren, and Merrill Moore celebrated the South in their verse and prose.

In New York City, Harlem became an exciting literary and artistic center during the twenties. Originally a white suburb, economic and racial segregation had transformed Harlem into a ghetto. In an effort to bring the Black community to a fuller appreciation of its own cultural heritage and identity, and to demonstrate their achievements to white America, Black intellectuals launched the so-called "Harlem Renaissance." The movement extended beyond writers and artists to include historians and sociologists as well. Magazines such as *Opportunity: A Journal of Negro Life* were founded to encourage talented Black writers. During this time, such important poets as Countee Cullen, James Weldon Johnson, and Langston Hughes arose. Cullen was the most traditional of the three, finding his models in the greats of English poetry. Johnson modelled the poems in his finest volume, *God's Trombones*, on old Black plantation sermons. Hughes ("The Poet Laureate of Harlem") couched his poems in the rhythms of jazz and blues. Each of these men made moving, powerful statements against the atrocities and indignities thrusted upon Blacks by a white society. Joining these voices of social protest were white poets, such as E. E. Cummings and Kenneth Fearing, who attacked materialism, moral hypocrisy, warfare, and conformity, in addition to racial prejudice.

Thus the years between the two World Wars saw the continued development of modern American verse, as poets explored their personal and ancestral identities, their roles and responsibilities as artists and citizens, and the problems and challenges of the twentieth century. It is a rich and distinguished period of American letters, one that well rewards either the serious student or the casual reader.

EXPLANATORY NOTES

The present anthology is arranged chronologically. Its aim is (a) to provide the reader with a sense of the development of verse during the historical period and (b) to help place select works within the span of each poet's creative output. Accordingly, it lists the poets in sequence—by date of birth—and, wherever possible, gives the date of individual poems.

Words are spelled as they appear in the original sources; punctuation, capitalization, and usage are treated the same way. No attempt has been made to reconcile resulting inconsistencies. This, however, should not hinder a basic appreciation of the material. In some cases, the poems entered constitute selections; these are chosen to convey to the reader the essence of a major work which is too long to publish in the context of the anthology.

Authors, titles, and first lines are arranged in a single alphabetical listing in the Index. Poet names are in boldface; poem titles are in italics; and poem first lines are enclosed in quotation marks. When a title and first line are identical, only the title is given.

JAMES WELDON JOHNSON [1871–1938]

James Weldon Johnson was born in Jacksonville, Florida. He was educated at both Atlanta University and Columbia University and eventually became principal of the grammar school he had attended as a child. In 1901 he moved to New York, where he collaborated with his brother in writing songs, musicals, and material for vaudeville. From 1906 to 1913, he served as the United States Consul in Venezuela and Nicaragua, and he subsequently became secretary of the NAACP, a position he held until 1930.

Johnson did not publish his first book of verse until 1918 nor is it for this rather weak and clichéd effort that he is remembered. His most important achievement was a book of seven verse sermons that he published in 1927, entitled *God's Trombones*. Johnson had been impressed with the work of playwright John Synge, who portrayed the essential dignity and strength of the Irish peasant; Johnson hoped to do the same for the Blacks. His book caused quite a sensation when it first appeared, and it received much acclaim. Several years earlier, Johnson compiled the first American anthology of Black verse, entitled *The Book of American Negro Poetry* (1922). With his brother, he also edited two collections of Black spirituals.

O Black and Unknown Bards

O black and unknown bards of long ago,
How came your lips to touch the sacred fire?
How, in your darkness, did you come to know
The power and beauty of the minstrel's lyre?
Who first from midst his bonds lifted his eyes?
Who first from out the still watch, lone and long,
Feeling the ancient faith of prophets rise
Within his dark-kept soul, burst into song?

Heart of what slave poured out such melody
As "Steal away to Jesus"? On its strains
His spirit must have nightly floated free,
Though still about his hands he felt his chains.
Who heard great "Jordan roll"? Whose starward eye
Saw chariot "swing low"? And who was he
That breathed that comforting, melodic sigh,
"Nobody knows de trouble I see"?

What merely living clod, what captive thing,
Could up toward God through all its darkness grope,
And find within its deadened heart to sing
These songs of sorrow, love and faith, and hope?
How did it catch that subtle undertone,
That note in music heard not with the ears?
How sound the elusive reed so seldom blown,
Which stirs the soul or melts the heart to tears.

Not that great German master in his dream
Of harmonies that thundered amongst the stars
At the creation, ever heard a theme
Nobler than "Go down, Moses." Mark its bars
How like a mighty trumpet-call they stir
The blood. Such are the notes that men have sung
Going to valorous deeds; such tones there were
That helped make history when Time was young.

There is a wide, wide wonder in it all,
That from degraded rest and servile toil
The fiery spirit of the seer should call
These simple children of the sun and soil.
O black slave singers, gone, forgot, unfamed,
You–you alone, of all the long, long line
Of those who've sung untaught, unknown, unnamed,
Have stretched out upward, seeking the divine.

You sang not deeds of heroes or of kings;
No chant of bloody war, no exulting paean
Of arms-won triumphs; but your humble strings
You touched in chord with music empyrean.
You sang far better than you knew; the songs
That for your listeners' hungry hearts sufficed
Still live,–but more than this to you belongs:
You sang a race from wood and stone to Christ.

The Creation

A Negro Sermon

And God stepped out on space,
And He looked around and said,
"I'm lonely
I'll make me a world."

And as far as the eye of God could see
Darkness covered everything,
Blacker than a hundred midnights
Down in a cypress swamp.

Then God smiled,
And the light broke,
And the darkness rolled up on one side,
And the light stood shining on the other,
And God said, *"That's good!"*

Then God reached out and took the light in His hands,
And God rolled the light around in His hands
Until He made the sun;
And He set that sun a-blazing in the heavens.
And the light that was left from making the sun
God gathered it up in a shining ball
And flung it against the darkness,
Spangling the night with the moon and stars.
Then down between
The darkness and the light
He hurled the world;
And God said, *"That's good."*

Then God Himself stepped down–
And the sun was on His right hand
And the moon was on His left;
The stars were clustered about His head,
And the earth was under His feet.
And God walked, and where He trod
His footsteps hollowed the valleys out
And bulged the mountains up.
Then He stopped and looked, and saw
That the earth was hot and barren.
So God stepped over to the edge of the world
And He spat out the seven seas;
He batted His eyes, and the lightnings flashed;
He clapped His hands, and the thunders rolled;
And the waters above the earth came down,
The cooling waters came down.

Then the green grass sprouted,
And the little red flowers blossomed,
The pine tree pointed his finger to the sky,
And the oak spread out his arms,
And the lakes cuddled down in the hollows of the ground,
And the rivers ran to the sea;
And God smiled again,
And the rainbow appeared,
And curled itself around His shoulder.

Then God raised His arm and He waved His hand,
Over the sea and over the land,
And He said, *"Bring forth. Bring forth."*
And quicker than God could drop His hand
Fishes and fowls
And beasts and birds
Swam the rivers and the seas,
Roamed the forests and the woods,
And split the air with their wings.
And God said, *"That's good."*

Then God walked around,
And God looked around
On all that He had made.
He looked at His sun,
And He looked at His moon,
And He looked at His little stars;
He looked on His world,
With all its living things,
And God said, *"I'm lonely still."*

Then God sat down
On the side of a hill where He could think;
By a deep, wide river He sat down;
With His head in His hands,
God thought and thought,
Till He thought, *"I'll make me a man."*

Up from the bed of a river
God scooped the clay;
And by the bank of the river
He kneeled Him down;
And there the great God Almighty
Who lit the sun and fixed it in the sky,
Who flung the stars to the most far corner of the night,
Who rounded the earth in the middle of His hand;
This Great God,
Like a mammy bending over her baby,
Kneeled down in the dust

Toiling over a lump of clay
Till He shaped it in His own image;

Then into it He blew the breath of life,
And man became a living soul.
Amen. Amen.

Go Down Death

A Funeral Sermon

Weep not, weep not,
She is not dead;
She's resting in the bosom of Jesus.
Heart-broken husband–weep no more;
Grief-stricken son–weep no more;
She's only just gone home.

Day before yesterday morning,
God was looking down from his great, high heaven,
Looking down on all his children,
And his eye fell on Sister Caroline,
Tossing on her bed of pain.
And God's big heart was touched with pity,
With the everlasting pity.

And God sat back on his throne,
And he commanded that tall, bright angel standing at his right hand:
Call me Death!
And that tall, bright angel cried in a voice
That broke like a clap of thunder:
Call Death!–Call Death!
And the echo sounded down the streets of heaven
Till it reached away back to that shadowy place,
Where Death waits with his pale, white horses.

And Death heard the summons,

And he leaped on his fastest horse,
Pale as a sheet in the moonlight.
Up the golden street Death galloped,
And the hoof of his horse struck fire from the gold,
But they didn't make no sound.
Up Death rode to the Great White Throne,
And waited for God's command.

And God said: Go down, Death, go down,
Go down to Savannah, Georgia,
Down in Yamacraw,
And find Sister Caroline.
She's borne the burden and heat of the day,
She's labored long in my vineyard,
And she's tired–
She's weary–
Go down, Death, and bring her to me.

And Death didn't say a word,
But he loosed the reins on his pale, white horse,
And he clamped the spurs to his bloodless sides,
And out and down he rode,
Through heaven's pearly gates,
Past suns and moons and stars;
On Death rode,
And the foam from his horse was like a comet in the sky;
On Death rode,
Leaving the lightning's flash behind;
Straight on down he came.

While we were watching round her bed,
She turned her eyes and looked away,
She saw what we couldn't see;
She saw Old Death. She saw Old Death.
Coming like a falling star.
But Death didn't frighten Sister Caroline;
He looked to her like a welcome friend.
And she whispered to us: I'm going home,
And she smiled and closed her eyes.

And Death took her up like a baby,
And she lay in his icy arms,
But she didn't feel no chill.
And Death began to ride again–
Up beyond the evening star,
Out beyond the morning star,
Into the glittering light of glory,
On to the Great White Throne.
And there he laid Sister Caroline
On the loving breast of Jesus.

And Jesus took his own hand and wiped away her tears,
And he smoothed the furrows from her face,
And the angels sang a little song,
And Jesus rocked her in his arms,
And kept a-saying: Take your rest,
Take your rest, take your rest.

WALLACE STEVENS [1879-1955]

Wallace Stevens was born and raised in Reading, Pennsylvania. He entered Harvard University as a special student in 1897, studying French and German and coming under the influence of George Santayana, the noted philosopher and poet. Stevens became president of the *Harvard Advocate*, in which—along with the *Harvard Monthly*—he published his own poems and stories. Upon graduation, he found work as a reporter on the New York *Tribune* but was ill-suited to a journalistic career. On the advice of his father, Stevens entered New York Law School and, in 1904, was admitted to the bar. Initially, he had little success practicing law, but, in 1908, he joined the legal staff of an insurance company and became confident enough of his financial security to marry Elsie Moll the following year. In 1916, he joined the Hartford Accident and Insurance Company and, soon thereafter, moved to Connecticut, where he lived the rest of his life.

Stevens first began to publish his poetry, as early as 1913, in little magazines such as Harriet Monroe's *Poetry* and Alfred Kreymborg's *Others*. He developed close friendships with Marianne Moore and William Carlos Williams but always remained a peripheral figure on the literary scene. Extremely critical of his own work, Stevens refused to publish a volume of his poems until 1923, with *Harmonium*. However, when his daughter Holly was born in the next year, Stevens ceased writing and devoted himself fully to his duties as a father and businessman. It was not until the early thirties that he resumed his literary endeavors. Some of the volumes which distinguished this later period include *Ideas of Order* (1935), *The Man With the Blue Guitar (1937), Parts of a World* (1942), and *Auroras of Autumn* (1950).

Stevens was a delicate stylist, and his verse is a celebration of the senses, a pageant of exquisitely-rendered impressions. He was fascinated with exotic words and syllables, and his language, at times, seems to drift into the realm of pure music. He sought the "beauty of inflections" and "innuendos", and perhaps no other poet was so sensitive to the shades and gradations of experience. He was awarded the Bollingen Prize in 1950, and the National Book Award and Pulitzer Prize in 1955, the year he died.

Sunday Morning

I

Complacencies of the peignoir, and late
Coffee and oranges in a sunny chair,
And the green freedom of a cockatoo
Upon a rug mingle to dissipate
The holy hush of ancient sacrifice.
She dreams a little, and she feels the dark
Encroachment of that old catastrophe,
As a calm darkens among water-lights.
The pungent oranges and bright, green wings
Seem things in some procession of the dead,
Winding across wide water, without sound.
The day is like wide water, without sound,
Stilled for the passing of her dreaming feet
Over the seas, to silent Palestine,
Dominion of the blood and sepulchre.

II

Why should she give her bounty to the dead?
What is divinity if it can come
Only in silent shadows and in dreams?
Shall she not find in comforts of the sun,
In pungent fruit and bright, green wings, or else
In any balm or beauty of the earth,
Things to be cherished like the thought of heaven?
(Divinity must live within herself:)
Passions of rain, or moods in falling snow;
Grievings in loneliness, or unsubdued
Elations when the forest blooms; gusty
Emotions on wet roads on autumn nights;
All pleasures and all pains, remembering
The bough of summer and the winter branch.
These are the measures destined for her soul.

III

Jove in the clouds had his inhuman birth.
No mother suckled him, no sweet land gave
Large-mannered motions to his mythy mind.
He moved among us, as a muttering king,
Magnificent, would move among his hinds,
Until our blood, commingling, virginal,
With heaven, brought such requital to desire
The very hinds discerned it, in a star.
Shall our blood fail? Or shall it come to be
The blood of paradise? And shall the earth
Seem all of paradise that we shall know?
The sky will be much friendlier then than now,
A part of labor and a part of pain,
And next in glory to enduring love,
Not this dividing and indifferent blue.

IV

She says, "I am content when wakened birds,
Before they fly, test the reality
Of misty fields, by their sweet questionings;
But when the birds are gone, and their warm fields
Return no more, where, then, is paradise?"
There is not any haunt of prophecy,
Nor any old chimera of the grave,
Neither the golden underground, nor isle
Melodious, where spirits gat them home,
Nor visionary south, nor cloudy palm
Remote on heaven's hill, that has endured
As April's green endures; or will endure
Like her remembrance of awakened birds,
Or her desire for June and evening, tipped
By the consummation of the swallow's wings.

V

She says, "But in contentment I still feel
The need of some imperishable bliss."
Death is the mother of beauty; hence from her,
Alone, shall come fulfillment to our dreams
And our desires. Although she strews the leaves
Of sure obliteration on our paths,
The path sick sorrow took, the many paths
Where triumph rang its brassy phrase, or love
Whispered a little out of tenderness,
She makes the willow shiver in the sun
For maidens who were wont to sit and gaze
Upon the grass, relinquished to their feet.
She causes boys to pile new plums and pears
On disregarded plate. The maidens taste
And stray impassioned in the littering leaves.

VI

Is there no change of death in paradise?
Does ripe fruit never fall? Or do the boughs
Hang always heavy in that perfect sky,
Unchanging, yet so like our perishing earth,
With rivers like our own that seek for seas
They never find, the same receding shores
That never touch with inarticulate pang?
Why set the pear upon those river-banks
Or spice the shores with odors of the plum?
Alas, that they should wear our colors there,
The silken weavings of our afternoons,
And pick the strings of our insipid lutes!
Death is the mother of beauty, mystical,
Within whose burning bosom we devise
Our earthly mothers waiting, sleeplessly.

VII

Supple and turbulent, a ring of men
Shall chant in orgy on a summer morn
Their boisterous devotion to the sun,
Not as a god, but as a god might be,
Naked among them, like a savage source.
Their chant shall be a chant of paradise,
Out of their blood, returning to the sky;
And in their chant shall enter, voice by voice,
The windy lake wherein their lord delights,
The trees, like serafin, and echoing hills,
That choir among themselves long afterward.
They shall know well the heavenly fellowship
Of men that perish and of summer morn.
And whence they came and whither they shall go
The dew upon their feet shall manifest.

VIII

She hears, upon that water without sound,
A voice that cries, "The tomb in Palestine
Is not the porch of spirits lingering.
It is the grave of Jesus, where he lay."
We live in an old chaos of the sun,
Or old dependency of day and night,
Or island solitude, unsponsored, free,
Of that wide water, inescapable.
Deer walk upon our mountains, and the quail
Whistle about us their spontaneous cries;
Sweet berries ripen in the wilderness;
And, in the isolation of the sky,
At evening, casual flocks of pigeons make
Ambiguous undulations as they sink,
Downward to darkness, on extended wings.

Disillusionment of Ten O'Clock

The houses are haunted
By white night-gowns.
None are green,
Or purple with green rings,
Or green with yellow rings,
Or yellow with blue rings.
None of them are strange,
With socks of lace
And beaded ceintures.
People are not going
To dream of baboons and periwinkles.
Only, here and there, an old sailor,
Drunk and asleep in his boots,
Catches tigers
In red weather.

*Thirteen Ways of Looking
at a Blackbird*

I

Among twenty snowy mountains,
The only moving thing
Was the eye of the blackbird.

II

I was of three minds,
Like a tree
In which there are three blackbirds.

III

The blackbird whirled in the autumn winds.
It was a small part of the pantomime.

IV

A man and a woman
Are one.
A man and a woman and a blackbird
Are one.

V

I do not know which to prefer,
The beauty of inflections
Or the beauty of innuendoes,
The blackbird whistling
Or just after.

VI

Icicles filled the long window
With barbaric glass.
The shadow of the blackbird
Crossed it, to and fro.
The mood
Traced in the shadow
An indecipherable cause.

VII

O thin men of Haddam,
Why do you imagine golden birds?
Do you not see how the blackbird
Walks around the feet
Of the women about you?

VIII

I know noble accents
And lucid, inescapable rhythms;
But I know, too,
That the blackbird is involved
In what I know.

IX

When the blackbird flew out of sight,
It marked the edge
Of one of many circles.

X

At the sight of blackbirds
Flying in a green light,
Even the bawds of euphony
Would cry out sharply.

XI

He rode over Connecticut
In a glass coach.
Once, a fear pierced him,
In that he mistook
The shadow of his equipage
For blackbirds.

XII

The river is moving.
The blackbird must be flying.

XIII

It was evening all afternoon.
It was snowing
And it was going to snow.
The blackbird sat
In the cedar-limbs.

Metaphors of a Magnifico

Twenty men crossing a bridge,
Into a village,
Are twenty men crossing twenty bridges,
Into twenty villages,
Or one man
Crossing a single bridge into a village.

This is old song
That will not declare itself . . .

Twenty men crossing a bridge,
Into a village,

Are
Twenty men crossing a bridge
Into a village.

That will not declare itself
Yet is certain as meaning . . .

The boots of the men clump
On the boards of the bridge.
The first white wall of the village
Rises through fruit-trees.

Of what was it I was thinking?

So the meaning escapes.

The first white wall of the village . . .
The fruit-trees. . . .

Anecdote of the Jar

I placed a jar in Tennessee,
And round it was, upon a hill.
It made the slovenly wilderness
Surround that hill.

The wilderness rose up to it,
And sprawled around, no longer wild.
The jar was round upon the ground
And tall and of a port in air.

It took dominion everywhere.
The jar was gray and bare.
It did not give of bird or bush,
Like nothing else in Tennessee.

A High-Toned Old Christian Woman

Poetry is the supreme fiction, madame.
Take the moral law and make a nave of it
And from the nave build haunted heaven. Thus,
The conscience is converted into palms,
Like windy citherns hankering for hymns.
We agree in principle. That's clear. But take
The opposing law and make a peristyle,
And from the peristyle project a masque
Beyond the planets. Thus, our bawdiness,
Unpurged by epitaph, indulged at last,
Is equally converted into palms,
Squiggling like saxophones. And palm for palm,
Madame, we are where we began. Allow,
Therefore, that in the planetary scene
Your disaffected flagellants, well-stuffed,
Smacking their muzzy bellies in parade,
Proud of such novelties of the sublime,
Such tink and tank and tunk-a-tunk-tunk,

May, merely may, madame, whip from themselves
A jovial hullabaloo among the spheres.
This will make widows wince. But fictive things
Wink as they will. Wink most when widows wince.

The Emperor of Ice-Cream

Call the roller of big cigars,
The muscular one, and bid him whip
In kitchen cups concupiscent curds.
Let the wenches dawdle in such dress
As they are used to wear, and let the boys
Bring flowers in last month's newspapers.
Let be be finale of seem.
The only emperor is the emperor of ice-cream.

Take from the dresser of deal,
Lacking the three glass knobs, that sheet
On which she embroidered fantails once
And spread it so as to cover her face.
If her horny feet protrude, they come
To show how cold she is, and dumb.
Let the lamp affix its beam.
The only emperor is the emperor of ice-cream.

The Idea of Order at Key West

She sang beyond the genius of the sea.
The water never formed to mind or voice,
Like a body wholly body, fluttering
Its empty sleeves; and yet its mimic motion
Made constant cry, caused constantly a cry,
That was not ours although we understood,
Inhuman, of the veritable ocean.

The sea was not a mask. No more was she.
The song and water were not medleyed sound
Even if what she sang was what she heard,
Since what she sang was uttered word by word.
It may be that in all her phrases stirred
The grinding water and the gasping wind;
But it was she and not the sea we heard.

For she was the maker of the song she sang.
The ever-hooded, tragic-gestured sea
Was merely a place by which she walked to sing.
Whose spirit is this? we said, because we knew
It was the spirit that we sought and knew
That we should ask this often as she sang.

If it was only the dark voice of the sea
That rose, or even colored by many waves;
If it was only the outer voice of sky
And cloud, of the sunken coral water-walled,
However clear, it would have been deep air,
The heaving speech of air, a summer sound
Repeated in a summer without end
And sound alone. But it was more than that,
More even than her voice, and ours, among
The meaningless plungings of water and the wind,
Theatrical distances, bronze shadows heaped
On high horizons, mountainous atmospheres
Of sky and sea.

                    It was her voice that made
The sky acutest at its vanishing.
She measured to the hour its solitude.
She was the single artificer of the world
In which she sang. And when she sang, the sea,
Whatever self it had, became the self
That was her song, for she was the maker. Then we,
As we beheld her striding there alone,
Knew that there never was a world for her
Except the one she sang and, singing, made.

Ramon Fernandez, tell me, if you know,
Why, when the singing ended and we turned
Toward the town, tell why the glassy lights,
The lights in the fishing boats at anchor there,
As the night descended, tilting in the air,
Mastered the night and portioned out the sea,
Fixing emblazoned zones and fiery poles,
Arranging, deepening, enchanting night.

Oh! Blessed rage for order, pale Ramon,
The maker's rage to order words of the sea,
Words of the fragrant portals, dimly-starred,
And of ourselves and of our origins,
In ghostlier demarcations, keener sounds.

Evening Without Angels

the great interests of man: air and
light, the joy of having a body, the
voluptuousness of looking.
                                        –MARIO ROSSI

Why seraphim like lutanists arranged
Above the trees? And why the poet as
Eternal *chef d'orchestre*?

                    Air is air.
Its vacancy glitters round us everywhere.
Its sounds are not angelic syllables
But our unfashioned spirits realized
More sharply in more furious selves.

                    And light
That fosters seraphim and is to them
Coiffeur of haloes, fecund jeweller–
Was the sun concoct for angels or for men?
Sad men made angels of the sun, and of

The moon they made their own attendant ghosts,
Which led them back to angels, after death.

Let this be clear that we are men of sun
And men of day and never of pointed night,
Men that repeat antiquest sounds of air
In an accord of repetitions. Yet,
If we repeat, it is because the wind
Encircling us, speaks always with our speech

Light, too, encrusts us making visible
The motions of the mind and giving form
To moodiest nothings, as, desire for day
Accomplished in the immensely flashing East,
Desire for rest, in that descending sea
Of dark, which in its very darkening
Is rest and silence spreading into sleep.

. . . Evening, when the measure skips a beat
And then another, one by one, and all
To a seething minor swiftly modulate.
Bare night is best. Bare earth is best. Bare, bare,
Except for our own houses, huddled low
Beneath the arches and their spangled air,
Beneath the rhapsodies of fire and fire,
Where the voice that is in us makes a true response,
Where the voice that is great within us rises up,
As we stand gazing at the rounded moon.

Of Modern Poetry

The poem of the mind in the act of finding
What will suffice. It has not always had
To find: the scene was set; it repeated what
Was in the script.
                    Then the theatre was changed
To something else. Its past was a souvenir.

It has to be living, to learn the speech of the place.
It has to face the men of the time and to meet
The women of the time. It has to think about war
And it has to find what will suffice. It has
To construct a new stage. It has to be on that stage
And, like an insatiable actor, slowly and
With meditation, speak words that in the ear,
In the delicatest ear of the mind, repeat,
Exactly, that which it wants to hear, at the sound
Of which, an invisible audience listens,
Not to the play, but to itself, expressed
In an emotion as of two people, as of two
Emotions becoming one. The actor is
A metaphysician in the dark, twanging
An instrument, twanging a wiry string that gives
Sounds passing through sudden rightnesses, wholly
Containing the mind, below which it cannot descend,
Beyond which it has no will to rise.
                                    It must
Be the finding of satisfaction, and may
Be of a man skating, a woman dancing, a woman
Combing. The poem of the act of the mind.

Mrs. Alfred Uruguay

So what said the others and the sun went down
And, in the brown blues of evening, the lady said,
In the donkey's ear, "I fear that elegance
Must struggle like the rest." She climbed until
The moonlight in her lap, (mewing) her velvet,
And her dress were one and said, "I have said no
To everything, in order to get at myself.
I have wiped away moonlight like mud. Your innocent ear
And I, if I rode naked, are what remain."

The moonlight crumbled to degenerate forms,
While she approached the real, upon her mountain,

With lofty darkness. The donkey was there to ride,
To hold by the ear, even though it wished for a bell,
Wished faithfully for a falsifying bell.
Neither the moonlight could change it. And for her,
To be, regardless of velvet, could never be more
Than to be, she could never differently be,
Her no and no made yes impossible.

Who was it passed her there on a horse all will,
What figure of capable imagination?
Whose horse clattered on the road on which she rose,
As it descended, blind to her velvet and
The moonlight? Was it a rider intent on the sun,
A youth, a lover with phosphorescent hair,
Dressed poorly, arrogant of his streaming forces,
Lost in an integration of the martyrs' bones,
Rushing from what was real; and capable?

The villages slept as the capable man went down,
Time swished on the village clocks and dreams were alive,
The enormous gongs gave edges to their sounds,
As the rider, no chevalere and poorly dressed,
Impatient of the bells and midnight forms,
Rode over the picket rocks, rode down the road,
And, capable, created in his mind,
Eventual victor, out of the martyrs' bones,
The ultimate elegance: the imagined land.

Dutch Graves in Bucks County

Angry men and furious machines
Swarm from the little blue of the horizon
To the great blue of the middle height.
Men scatter throughout clouds.
The wheels are too large for any noise.

And you, my semblables, in sooty residence
Tap skeleton drums inaudibly.
There are shouts and voices.
There are men shuffling on foot in air.
Men are moving and marching
And shuffling lightly, with the heavy lightness
Of those that are marching, many together.

And you, my semblables—the old flag of Holland
Flutters in tiny darkness.

There are circles of weapons in the sun.
The air attends the brightened guns,
As if sounds were forming
Out of themselves, a saying,
An expressive on-dit, a profession.

And you, my semblables, are doubly killed
To be buried in desert and deserted earth.

The flags are natures newly found.
Rifles grow sharper on the sight.
There is a rumble of autumnal marching,
From which no soft sleeve relieves us.
Fate is the present desperado.

And you, my semblables, are crusts that lie
In the shrivellings of your time and place.

There is a battering of the drums. The bugles
Cry loudly, cry out in the powerful heart.
A force gathers that will cry loudlier
Than the most metal music, loudlier,
Like an instinctive incantation.

And you, my semblables, in the total
Of remembrance share nothing of ourselves.

The Ultimate Poem Is Abstract

This day writhes with what? The lecturer
On This Beautiful World Of Ours composes himself
And hems the planet rose and haws it ripe,

And red, and right. The particular question–here
The particular answer to the particular question
Is not in point–the question is in point.

If the day writhes, it is not with revelations.
One goes on asking questions. That, then, is one
Of the categories. So said, this placid space

Is changed. It is not so blue as we thought. To be blue,
There must be no questions. It is an intellect
Of windings round and dodges to and fro,

An end must come in a merciless triumph,
An end of evil in a profounder logic,
In a peace that is more than a refuge,
In the will of what is common to all men,
Spelled from spent living and spent dying.

And you, my semblables, in gaffer-green,
Know that the past is not part of the present.

There were other soldiers, other people,
Men came as the sun comes, early children
And late wanderers creeping under the barb of night,
Year, year and year, defeated at last and lost
In an ignorance of sleep with nothing won.

And you, my semblables, know that this time
Is not an early time that has grown late.

But these are not those rusted armies.
There are the lewdest and the lustiest,
The hullaballoo of health and have,

The much too many disinherited
In a storm of torn-up testaments.

And you, my semblables, know that your children
Are not your children, not your selves.

Who are the mossy cronies muttering,
Monsters antique and haggard with past thought?
What is this crackling of voices in the mind,
This pitter-patter of archaic freedom,
Of the thousands of freedoms except our own?

And you, my semblables, whose ecstasy
Was the glory of heaven in the wilderness—

Freedom is like a man who kills himself
Each night, an incessant butcher, whose knife
Grows sharp in blood. The armies kill themselves,
And in their blood an ancient evil dies—
The action of incorrigible tragedy.

And you, my semblables, behold in blindness
That a new glory of new men assembles.

This is the pit of torment that placid end
Should be illusion, that the mobs of birth
Avoid our stale perfections, seeking out
Their own, waiting until we go
To picnic in the ruins that we leave.

So that the stars, my semblables, chimeres,
Shine on the very living of those alive.

These violent marchers of the present,
Rumbling along the autumnal horizon,
Under the arches, over the arches, in arcs
Of a chaos composed in more than order,
March toward a generation's centre.

Time was not wasted in your subtle temples.
No: nor divergence made too steep to follow down.

Writhings in wrong obliques and distances,
Not an intellect in which we are fleet: present
Everywhere in space at once, cloud-pole

Of communication. It would be enough
If we were ever, just once, at the middle, fixed
In This Beautiful World Of Ours and not as now,

Helplessly at the edge, enough to be
Complete, because at the middle, if only in sense,
And in that enormous sense, merely enjoy.

The Sail of Ulysses

Under the shape of his sail, Ulysses,
Symbol of the seeker, crossing by night
The giant sea, read his own mind.
He said, "As I know, I am and have
The right to be." Guiding his boat
Under the middle stars, he said:

I

"If knowledge and the thing known are one
So that to know a man is to be
That man, to know a place is to be
That place, and it seems to come to that;
And if to know one man is to know all
And if one's sense of a single spot
Is what one knows of the universe,
Then knowledge is the only life,
The only sun of the only day,
The only access to true ease,
The deep comfort of the world and fate.

II

There is a human loneliness,
A part of space and solitude,
In which knowledge cannot be denied,
In which nothing of knowledge fails,
The luminous companion, the hand,
The fortifying arm, the profound
Response, the completely answering voice,
That which is more than anything else
The right within us and about us,
Joined, the triumphant vigor, felt,
The inner direction on which we depend,
That which keeps us the little that we are,
The aid of greatness to be and the force.

III

This is the true creator, the waver
Waving purpling wands, the thinker
Thinking gold thoughts in a golden mind,
Loftily jingled, radiant,
The joy of meaning in design
Wrenched out of chaos . . . The quiet lamp
For this creator is a lamp
Enlarging like a nocturnal ray
The space in which it stands, the shine
Of darkness, creating from nothingness
Such black constructions, such public shapes
And murky masonry, one wonders
At the finger that brushes this aside
Gigantic in everything but size.

IV

The unnamed creator of an unknown sphere,
Unknown as yet, unknowable,
Uncertain certainty, Apollo
Imagined among the indigenes

And Eden conceived on Morningside,
The centre of the self, the self
Of the future, of future man
And future place, when these are known,
A freedom at last from the mystical,
The beginning of a final order,
The order of man's right to be
As he is, the discipline of his scope
Observed as an absolute, himself.

V

A longer, deeper breath sustains
The eloquence of right, since knowing
And being are one: the right to know
And the right to be are one. We come
To knowledge when we come to life.
Yet always there is another life,
A life beyond this present knowing,
A life lighter than this present splendor,
Brighter, perfected and distant away,
Not to be reached but to be known,
Not an attainment of the will
But something illogically received,
A divination, a letting down
From loftiness, misgivings dazzlingly
Resolved in dazzling discovery.
There is no map of paradise.
The great Omnium descends on us
As a free race. We know it, one
By one, in the right of all. Each man
Is an approach to the vigilance
In which the litter of truths becomes
A whole, the day on which the last star
Has been counted, the genealogy
Of gods and men destroyed, the right
To know established as the right to be.
The ancient symbols will be nothing then.
We shall have gone behind the symbols

To that which they symbolized, away
From the rumors of the speech-full domes,
To the chatter that is then the true legend,
Like glitter ascended into fire.

VI

Master of the world and of himself,
He came to this by knowledge or
Will come. His mind presents the world
And in his mind the world revolves.
The revolutions through day and night,
Through wild spaces of other suns and moons,
Round summer and angular winter and winds,
Are matched by other revolutions
In which the world goes round and round
In the crystal atmospheres of the mind,
Light's comedies, dark's tragedies,
Like things produced by a climate, the world
Goes round in the climates of the mind
And bears its floraisons of imagery.

The mind renews the world in a verse,
A passage of music, a paragraph
By a right philosopher: renews
And possesses by sincere insight
In the John-begat-Jacob of what we know,
The flights through space, changing habitudes.

In the generations of thought, man's sons
And heirs are powers of the mind,
His only testament and estate.
He has nothing but the truth to leave.
How then shall the mind be less than free
Since only to know is to be free?

VII

The living man in the present place,

Always, the particular thought
Among Plantagenet abstractions,
Always and always, the difficult inch
On which the vast arches of space
Repose, always, the credible thought
From which the incredible systems spring,
The little confine soon unconfined
In stellar largenesses–these things
Are the manifestations of a law
That bends the particulars to the abstract,
Makes them a pack on a giant's back,
A majestic mother's flocking brood,
As if abstractions were, themselves
Particulars of a relative sublime.
This is not poet's ease of mind.
It is the fate that dwells in truth.
We obey the coaxings of our end.

VIII

What is the shape of the sibyl? Not,
For a change, the englistered woman, seated
In colorings harmonious, dewed and dashed
By them: gorgeous symbol seated
On the seat of halidom, rainbowed,
Piercing the spirit by appearance,
A summing up of the loftiest lives
And their directing sceptre, the crown
And final effulgence and delving show.
It is the sibyl of the self,
The self as sibyl, whose diamond,
Whose chiefest embracing of all wealth
Is poverty, whose jewel found
At the exactest central of the earth
Is need. For this, the sibyl's shape
Is a blind thing fumbling for its form,
A form that is lame, a hand, a back,
A dream too poor, too destitute
To be remembered, the old shape

Worn and leaning to nothingness,
A woman looking down the road,
A child asleep in its own life.
As these depend, so must they use.
They measure the right to use. Need makes
The right to use. Need names on its breath
Categories of bleak necessity,
Which, just to name, is to create
A help, a right to help, a right
To know what helps and to attain,
By right of knowing, another plane.
The englistered woman is now seen
In an isolation, separate
From the human in humanity,
A part of the inhuman more,
The still inhuman more, and yet
An inhuman of our features, known
And unknown, inhuman for a little while,
Inhuman for a little, lesser time."

The great sail of Ulysses seemed,
In the breathings of this soliloquy,
Alive with an enigma's flittering . . .
As if another sail went on
Straight forwardly through another night
And clumped stars dangled all the way.

As You Leave the Room

You speak. You say: Today's character is not
A skeleton out of its cabinet. Nor am I.

That poem about the pineapple, the one
About the mind as never satisfied,

The one about the credible hero, the one
About summer, are not what skeletons think about.

I wonder, have I lived a skeleton's life,
As a disbeliever in reality,

A countryman of all the bones in the world?
Now, here, the snow I had forgotten becomes

Part of a major reality, part of
An appreciation of a reality

And thus an elevation, as if I left
With something I could touch, touch every way.

And yet nothing has been changed except what is
Unreal, as if nothing had been changed at all.

Of Mere Being

The palm at the end of the mind,
Beyond the last thought, rises
In the bronze decor,

A gold-feathered bird
Sings in the palm, without human meaning,
Without human feeling, a foreign song.

You know then that it is not the reason
That makes us happy or unhappy.
The bird sings. Its feathers shine.

The palm stands on the edge of space.
The wind moves slowly in the branches.
The bird's fire-fangled feathers dangle down.

ROBINSON JEFFERS [1887-1962]

Robinson Jeffers was born in Pittsburgh, Pennsylvania, where his father was a professor at the Western Theological Seminary. During his boyhood years, Jeffers studied on the continent before returning to the U.S. in 1903. He attended Occidental College in Los Angeles and graduated at age eighteen. In the following years, he studied variously at the University of Southern California, the University of Zurich, medical school in Los Angeles, and the University of Washington School of Forestry but found that none of these programs engaged him. His true interest, he discovered, was poetry. In 1912, after receiving a small legacy, he brought out his first book of poems, *Flagons and Apples*. By now he was deeply in love with the woman who was to be his life's companion, Una Call Kuster, and, in August of 1913, they were married. The two settled in the village of Carmel, California, where they spent the rest of their lives.

In 1925, *Tamar and Other Poems* was published by a small printer and caused something of an overnight sensation. In 1927, *The Women of Point Sur* appeared, in 1928, *Cawdor*. He was awarded a Book-of-the-Month Club Fellowship in 1937 for distinguished work over a period of time, and, in 1946, his loose translation of Euripides' *Medea* appeared on Broadway with Judith Anderson in the leading role. Jeffers was consumed with the epic verse form and time and again turned to classical and biblical subjects for inspiration. His poems view life through dismal, pessimistic eyes, and, indeed, his negativism can become oppressive. Nonetheless, the drama and power of his work is undeniable.

Age in Prospect

Praise youth's hot blood if you will, I think that happiness
Rather consists in having lived clear through
Youth and hot blood, on to the wintrier hemisphere
Where one has time to wait and to remember.

Youth and hot blood are beautiful, so is peacefulness.
Youth had some islands in it, but age is indeed
An island and a peak; age has infirmities,
Not few, but youth is all one fever.

To look around and to love in his appearances,
Though a little calmly, the universal God's
Beauty is better I think than to lip eagerly
The mother's breast or another woman's.

And there is no possession more sure than memory's;
But if I reach that gray island, that peak,
My hope is still to possess with eyes the homeliness
Of ancient loves, ocean and mountains,

And meditate the sea-mouth of mortality
And the fountain six feet down with a quieter thirst
Than now I feel for old age; a creature progressively
Thirsty for life will be for death too.

Ante Mortem

It is likely enough that lions and scorpions
Guard the end; life never was bonded to be endurable nor the act of dying
Unpainful; the brain burning too often
Earns, though it held itself detached from the object, often a burnt age.
No matter, I shall not shorten it by hand.
Incapable of body or unmoved of brain is no evil, one always went
      envying
The quietness of stones. But if the striped blossom

Insanity spread lewd splendors and lightning terrors at the end of the
    forest;
Or intolerable pain work its known miracle,
Exile the monarch soul, set a sick monkey in the office . . . remember me
Entire and balanced when I was younger,
And could lift stones, and comprehend in the praises the cruelties of life.

Post Mortem

Happy people die whole, they are all dissolved in a moment, they have
    had what they wanted,
No hard gifts; the unhappy
Linger a space, but pain is a thing that is glad to be forgotten; but one who
    has given
His heart to a cause or a country,
His ghost may spaniel it a while, disconsolate to watch it. I was wondering
    how long the spirit
That sheds this verse will remain
When the nostrils are nipped, when the brain rots in its vault or bubbles in
    the violence of fire
To be ash in metal. I was thinking
Some stalks of the wood whose roots I married to the earth of this place
    will stand five centuries;
I held the roots in my hand,
The stems of the trees between two fingers: how many remote
    generations of women
Will drink joy from men's loins,
And dragged from between the thighs of what mothers will giggle at my
    ghost when it curses the axemen,
Gray impotent voice on the sea-wind,
When the last trunk falls? The women's abundance will have built roofs
    over all this foreland;
Will have buried the rock foundations
I laid here: the women's exuberance will canker and fail in its time and
    like clouds the houses
Unframe, the granite of the prime

Stand from the heaps: come storm and wash clean: the plaster
    is all run to
All rusted; the foreland resumes
The form we loved when we saw it. Though one at the end of the age and
    far off from this place
Should meet my presence in a poem,
The ghost would not care but be here, long sunset shadow in the seams of
    granite, and forgotten
The flesh, a spirit for the stone.

Clouds of Evening

Enormous cloud-mountains that form over Point Lobos and into the
    sunset,
Figures of fire on the walls of tonight's storm,
Foam of gold in gorges of fire, and the great file of warrior angels:
Dreams gathering in the curdled brain of the earth—
The sky the brain-vault—on the threshold of sleep: poor earth, you, like
    your children
By inordinate desires tortured, make dreams?
Storms more enormous, wars nobler, more toppling mountains, more
    jeweled waters, more free
Fires on impossible headlands . . . as a poor girl
Wishing her lover taller and more desirous, and herself maned with gold,
Dreams the world right, in the cold bed, about dawn.
Dreams are beautiful; the slaves of form are beautiful also; I have
    grown to believe
A stone is a better pillow than many visions.

Apology for Bad Dreams

I

In the purple light, heavy with redwood, the slopes drop seaward,
Headlong convexities of forest, drawn in together to the steep ravice.

Below, on the sea-cliff,
A lonely clearing; a little field of corn by the streamside; a roof under
    spared trees. Then the ocean
Like a great stone someone has cut to a sharp edge and polished to
    shining. Beyond it, the fountain
And furnace of incredible light flowing up from the sunk sun.
    In the little clearing a woman
Is punishing a hors; she had tied the halter to a sapling at the edge of tyhe
    wood, but when the great whip
Clung to the flanks the creature kicked so hard she feared he would snap
    the halter; she called form the house
The young man her son; who fetched a chain tie-rope, they working
    together
        Noosed the small rusty links round the horse's tongue
        And tied him by the swollen tongue to the tree.
        Seen from this height they are shrunk to insect size.
        Out of all human relation. You cannot distinguish
        The blood dripping form where the cahin is fastened,
        The beast shuddering; but the thrust neck and the legs
        Far apart. You can see the whip fall on the flanks . . .
        The gesture of the arm. You cannot see the face of the woman.
        The enormous light beats up out of the west across the cloud-bars of
        the trade-wind. The ocean
Darkens, the high clounds brighten, the hills darken together. Unbridled
    and unbelievable beauty
Covers the evening world . . . not covers, grows apparent out of it, as
    Venus down there grows out
From the lit skyu. What said the prophet? "I create good: and I create evil:
    I am the Lord."

II

This coast crying out for tragedy like all beautiful places,
(The quiet ones ask for quieter suffering; but here the granite cliff the
    gaunt cypresses' crown
Demands what victim? The dykes of red lava and black what Titan?
    The hills like pointed flames
Beyond Soberanes, the terrible peaks of the bare hills under the sun, what
    immolation?)

This coast crying out for tragedy like all beautiful places: and like the
    passionate spirit of humanity
Pain for its bread: God's, many victims', the painful deaths, the horrible
    transfigurements: I said in my heart,
"Better invent than suffer: imagine victims
Lest your own flesh be chosen the agonist, or you
Martyr some creature to the beauty of the place." And I said,
"Burn sacrifices once a year to magic
Horror away from the house, this little house here
You have built over the ocean with your own hands
Beside the standing bowlders: for what are we,
The beast that walks upright, with speaking lips
And little hair, to think we should always be fed,
Sheltered, intact, and self-controlled? We sooner more liable
Than the other animals. Pain and terror, the insanities of desire; not
    accidents, but essential,
And crowd up from the core." I imagined victims for those wolves, I
    made the phantoms to follow.
They have hunted the phantoms and missed the house. It is not good to
    forget over what gulfs the spirit
Of the beauty of humanity, the petal of a lost flower blown seaward by the
    nightwind, floats to its quietness.

III

Bowlders blunted like an old bear's teeth break up from the headland;
    below them
All the soil is thick with shells, the tide-rock feasts of a dead people.
Here the granite flanks are scarred with ancient fire, the ghosts of the tribe
Crouch in the nights beside the ghost of a fire, they try to remember the
    sunlight,
Light has died out of their skies. These have paid something for the future
Luck of the country, while we living keep old griefs in memory: though
Luck of the country, while we living keep old griefs in memory: though
    God's
Sudden reminders from the cloud: remembered deaths be our redeemers;
Imagined victims our salvation: white as the half moon at midnight
Someone flamelike passed me, saying, "I am Tamar Cauldwell, I have
    my desire,"

Then the voice of the sea returned, when she had gone by, the stars to
    their towers.
. . . Beautiful country, burn again, Point Pinos down to the Sur Rivers
Burn as before with bitter wonders, land and ocean and the Carmel water.

IV

He brays humanity in a mortar to bring the savor
From the bruised root: a man having bad dreams, who invents victims,
    is only the ape of that God.
He washes it out with tears and many waters, calcines it with fire in the
    red crucible,
Deforms it, makes it horrible to itself: the spirit flies out and stands
    naked, he sees the spirit.
He takes it in the naked ecstasy; it breaks in his hand, the atom is broken,
    the power that massed it
Cries to the power that moves the stars, "I have come home to myself,
    behold me.
I bruised myself in the flint mortar and burnt me
In the red shell, I tortured myself, I flew forth,
Stood naked of myself and broke me in fragments,
And here am I moving the stars that are me."
I have seen these ways of God: I know of no reason
For fire and change and torture and the old returnings.
He being sufficient might be still. I think they admit no reason; they
    are the ways of my love.
Unmeasured power, incredible passion, enormous craft: no thought
    apparrent but burns darkly
Smothered with its own smoke in the human brain-vault: no thought
    outside: a certain measure in phenomena:
The fountains of the boiling stars, the flowers on the foreland, the ever-
    returning roses of dawn.

Night

The ebb slips from the rock, the sunken
Tide-rocks lift streaming shoulders
Out of the slack, the slow west
Sombering its torch; a ship's light
Shows faintly, far out,
Over the weight of the prone ocean
On the low cloud.

Over the dark mountain, over the dark pinewood,
Down the long dark valley along the shrunken river,
Returns the splendor without rays, the shining shadow,
Peace-bringer, the matrix of all shining and quieter of shining.
Where the shore widens on the bay she opens dark wings
And the ocean accepts her glory. O soul worshipful of her
You, like the ocean, have grave depths where she dwells always,
And the film of waves above that takes the sun takes also
Her, with more love. The sun-lovers have a blond favorite,
A father of lights and noises, wars, weeping and laughter,
Hot labor, lust and delight and the other blemishes.
     Quietness
Flows from her deeper fountain; and he will die; and she is immortal.

Far off from here the slender
Flocks of the mountain forest

Move among stems like towers
Of the old redwoods to stream,
No twig crackling; dip shy
Wild muzzles into the mountain water
Among the dark ferns.

O passionately at peace you being secure will pardon
The blasphemies of glowworms, the lamp in my tower, the fretfulness
Of cities, the crescents of the planets, the pride of the stars.
This August night in a rift of cloud Antares reddens,
The great one, the ancient torch, a lord among lost children,
The earth's orbit doubled would not girdle his greatness, one fire

Globed, out of grasp of the mind enormous; but to you
    O Night
What? Not a spark? What flicker of a spark in the faint far glimmer
Of a lost fire dying in the desert, dim coals of a sand-pit the Bedouins
Wandered from at dawn. . . . Ah singing prayer to what gulfs tempted
Suddenly are you more lost? To us the near-hand mountain
Be a measure of height, the tide-worn cliff at the sea-gate a measure of
    continuance.

The tide, moving the night's
Vastness with lonely voices,
Turns, the deep dark-shining
Pacific leans on the land,
Feeling his cold strength
To the outmost margins: you Night will resume
The stars in your time.

O passionately at peace when will that tide draw shoreward,
Truly the spouting fountains of light, Antares, Arcturus,
Tire of their flow, they sing one song but they think silence.
The striding winter-giant Orion shines, and dreams darkness.
And life, the flicker of men and moths and the wolf on the hill,
Though furious for continuance, passionately feeding, passionately
Remaking itself upon its mates, remembers deep inward
The calm mother, the quietness of the womb and the egg,
The primal and the latter silences: dear Night it is memory
Prophesies, prophecy that remembers, the charm of the dark.
And I and my people, we are willing to love the four-score years
Heartily; but as a sailor loves the sea, when the helm is for harbor.

Have men's minds changed,
Or the rock hidden in the deep of the waters of the soul
Broken the surface? A few centuries
Gone by, was none dared not to people
The darkness beyond the stars with harps and habitations.
But now, dear is the truth. Life is grown sweeter and lonelier,
And death is no evil.

Shine, Perishing Republic

While this America settles in the mold of its vulgarity, heavily
    thickening to empire,
And protest, only a bubble in the molten mass, popos and sighs out, and
    the mass hardens,

I sadly smiling remember that the flower fades to make fruit, the fruit
    rots to make earth.
Out of the mother; and through the spring exultances, ripeness and
    decadence; and home to the mother.

You making haste, haste on decay: not blameworthy; life is good, be it
    stubbornly long or suddenly
A mortal splendor: meteors are not needed less than mountains: shine,
    perishing republic.

But for my children, I would have them keep their distance from the
    thickening center; corruption
Never has been compulsory, when the cities lie at the monster's feet there
    the mountains.

And boys, be in nothing so moderate as in love of man, a clever servant,
    insufferable master.
There is the trap that catches noblest spirits, that caught–they say–God,
    when he walked on earth.

Hurt Hawks

I

The broken pillar of the wing jags from the clotted shoulder,
The wing trails like a banner in defeat,
No more to use the sky forever but live with famine
And pain a few days: cat nor coyote
Will shorten the week of waiting for death, there is game without talons.

He stands under the oak-bush and waits
The lame feet of salvation; at night he remembers freedom
And flies in a dream, the dawns ruin it.
He is strong and pain is worse to the strong, incapacity is worse.
The curs of the day come and torment him
At distance, no one but death the redeemer will humble that head,
The intrepid readiness, the terrible eyes.
The wild God of the world is sometimes merciful to those
That ask mercy, not often to the arrogant.
You do not know him, you communal people, or you have forgotten him;
Intemperate and savage, the hawk remembers him;
Beautiful and wild, the hawks, and men that are dying, remember him.

II

I'd sooner, except the penalties, kill a man than a hawk; but the great
    redtail
Had nothing left but unable misery
From the bone too shattered for mending, the wing that trailed under his
    talons when he moved.
We had fed him six weeks, I gave him freedom,
He wandered over the foreland hill and returned in the evening, asking
    for death,
Not like a beggar, still eyed with the old
Implacable arrogance. I gave him the lead gift in the twilight.
    What fell was relaxed,
Owl-downy, soft feminine feathers; but what
Soared: the fierce rush: the night-herons by the flooded river cried fear at
    its rising
Before it was quite unsheathed from reality.

New Mexican Mountain

I watch the Indians dancing to help the young corn at Taos pueblo.
    The old men squat in a ring
And make the song, the young women with fat bare arms, and a few
    shame-faced young men, shuffle the dance.

The lean-muscled young men are naked to the narrow loins, their
    breasts and backs daubed with white clay,
Two eagle-feathers plume the black heads. They dance with reluc-
    tance, they are growing civilized; the old men persuade them.

Only the drum is confident, it thinks the world has not changed; the
    beating heart, the simplest of rhythms,
It thinks the world has not changed at all; it is only a dreamer, a brain-
    less heart, the drum has no eyes.

These tourists have eyes, the hundred watching the dance, white
    Americans, hungrily too, with reverence, not laughter;
Pilgrims from civilization, anxiously seeking beauty, religion, poetry;
    pilgrims from the vacuum.

People from cities, anxious to be human again. Poor show how they
    suck you empty! The Indians are emptied,
And certainly there was never religion enough, nor beauty nor poetry
    here . . . to fill Americans.

Only the drum is confident, it thinks the world has not changed. Appar-
    ently only myself and the strong
Tribal drum, and the rockhead of Taos mountain, remember that
    civilization is a transient sickness.

Ave Caesar

No bitterness: our ancestors did it.
They were only ignorant and hopeful, they wanted freedom but wealth
    too.
Their children will learn to hope for a Caesar.
Or rather–for we are not aquiline Romans but soft mixed colonists–
Some kindly Sicilian tyrant who'll keep
Poverty and Carthage off until the Romans arrive.
We are easy to manage, a gregarious people,
Full of sentiment, clever at mechanics, and we love our luxuries.

MARIANNE MOORE   [1887-1972]

Marianne Moore was born in Kirkwood, Missouri to a devoutly Presbyterian family. Her father abandoned the family after his business collapsed, and, in 1894, she moved with her mother to Carlisle, Pennsylvania. Moore attended the Metzger Institute (where her mother taught) and, in 1909, graduated from Bryn Mawr College. Surprisingly, her forte was biology, not literature. Subsequently, she took courses at Carlisle Commercial College and, after travelling in England and France, taught stenography from 1911 to 1915 at the U.S. Indian School in Carlisle. In 1918, she moved to New York, where she worked variously as a private tutor, secretary, and assistant librarian. She had published poems in *Others*, *Poetry*, and *The Egoist* as early as 1915, but it was not until 1921 that her first volume of verse, *Poems*, appeared. (Actually, this book was published by admirers in London without her consent.) Between 1925 and 1929, she served as editor of *The Dial*, a leading review.

Perhaps Moore's greatest accomplishments came with *The Pangolin and Other Poems* (1936), *What Are Years?* (1941), and *Nevertheless* (1944). Her verse is distinguished by its precision, concision, and logic. She was a lover of Seventeenth Century English prose, and it has been remarked that her poetry often evinces the weight and directness of prose. In later years, she produced a translation of *The Fables of La Fontaine* (1954), and her *Collected Poems* (1951) received the National Book Award, as well as the Bollingen and Pulitzer prizes.

No Swan So Fine

"No water so still as the
    dead fountains of Versailles." No swan,
with swart blind look askance
and gondoliering legs, so fine
    as the chintz china one with fawn-
brown eyes and toothed gold
collar on to show whose bird it was.

Lodged in the Louis Fifteenth
    candelabrum-tree of cockscomb-
tinted buttons, dahlias,
sea-urchins, and everlastings,
    it perches on the branching foam
of polished sculptured
flowers–at ease and tall. The king is dead.

The Fish

wade
through black jade.
    Of the crow-blue mussel-shells, one keeps
    adjusting the ash-heaps;
        opening and shutting itself like

an
injured fan.
    The barnacles which encrust the side
    of the wave, cannot hide
        there for the submerged shafts of the

sun,
split like spun
    glass, move themselves with spotlight swiftness
    into the crevices–
        in and out, illuminating

the
turquoise sea
   of bodies. The water drives a wedge
   of iron through the iron edge
      of the cliff; whereupon the stars,

pink
rice-grains, ink-
   bespattered jelly-fish, crabs like green
   lilies, and submarine
      toadstools, slide each on the other.

All
external
   marks of abuse are present on this
   defiant edifice—
      all the physical features of

ac-
cident—lack
   of cornice, dynamite grooves, burns, and
   hatchet strokes, these things stand
      out on it; the chasm-side is

dead.
Repeated
   evidence has proved that it can live
   on what can not revive
      its youth. The sea grows old in it.

In This Age of Hard Trying, Nonchalance Is Good And

"really, it is not the
   business of the gods to bake clay pots." They did not
     do it in this instance. A few
        revolved upon the axes of their worth

as if excessive popularity might be a pot;

they did not venture the
     profession of humility. The polished wedge
          that might have split the firmament
               was dumb. At last it threw itself away
and falling down, conferred on some poor fool, a privilege.

"Taller by the length of
     a conversation of five hundred years than all
          the others," there was one, whose tales
               of what could never have been actual—
were better than the haggish, uncompanionable drawl

of certitude; his by-
     play was more terrible in its effectiveness
          than the fiercest frontal attack.
               The staff, the bag, the feigned inconsequence
of manner, best bespeak that weapon, self-protectiveness.

Critics and Connoisseurs

There is a great amount of poetry in unconscious
     fastidiousness. Certain Ming
          products, imperial floor coverings of coach-
wheel yellow, are well enough in their way but I have seen
          something
               that I like better—a
                    mere childish attempt to make an imperfectly ballasted
                         animal stand up,
                    similar determination to make a pup
                         eat his meat from the plate.

I remember a swan under the willows in Oxford,
     with flamingo-colored, maple-
          leaflike feet. It reconnoitered like a battle-
ship. Disbelief and conscious fastidiousness were the staple

ingredients in its
disinclination to move. Finally its hardihood was
not proof against its
proclivity to more fully appraise such bits
of food as the stream
bore counter to it; it made away with what I gave it
to eat. I have seen this swan and
I have seen you; I have seen ambition without
understanding in a variety of forms. Happening to stand
by an ant-hill, I have
seen a fastidious ant carrying a stick north, south,
east, west, till it turned on
itself, struck out from the flower-bed into the lawn,
and returned to the point

from which it had started. Then abandoning the stick as
useless and overtaxing its
jaws with a particle of whitewash–pill-like but
heavy, it again went through the same course of procedure.
What is
there in being able
to say that one has dominated the stream in an
attitude of self-defense;
in proving that one has had the experience
of carrying a stick?

The Monkeys

winked too much and were afraid of snakes. The zebras,
supreme in
their abnormality; the elephants with their fog-coloured skin
and strictly practical appendages
were there, the small cats; and the parakeet–
trivial and humdrum on examination, destroying
bark and portions of the food it could not eat.

I recall their magnificence, now not more magnificent
than it is dim. It is difficult to recall the ornament,
    speech, and precise manner of what one might
        call the minor acquaintances twenty
            years back; but I shall not forget him—that Gilgamesh
                among
        the hairy carnivora—that cat with the

wedge-shaped, slate-grey marks on its forelegs and the
            resolute tail,
astringently remarking, "They have imposed on us with their
                pale
    half-fledged protestations, trembling about
        in inarticulate frenzy, saying
            it is not for us to understand art; finding it
        all so difficult, examining the thing

as if it were inconceivably arcanic, as symmet-
rically frigid as if it had been carved out of chrysoprase
    or marble—strict with tension, malignant
        in its power over us and deeper
            than the sea when it proffers flattery in exchange for
                hemp,
        rye, flax, horses, platinum, timber, and fur."

                            England

with its baby rivers and little towns, each with its abbey or its
        cathedral,
with voices—one voice perhaps, echoing through the transept
        —the
criterion of suitability and convenience; and Italy with its equal
shores—contriving an epicureanism from which the grossness
        has been

extracted: and Greece with its goat and its gourds, the nest
    of modified illusions:

and France, the "chrysalis of the nocturnal butterfly," in
whose products mystery of construction diverts one from
    what was originally one's
object–substance at the core: and the East with its snails,
    its emotional

shorthand and jade cockroaches, its rock crystal and its im-
    perturbability,
all of museum quality: and America where there
is the little old ramshackle victoria in the south, where cigars
    are smoked on the
street in the north; where there are no proof-readers, no
    silk-worms, no digressions;

the wild man's land; grassless, linksless, languageless country
    in which letters are written
not in Spanish, not in Greek, not in Latin, not in shorthand,
but in plain American which cats and dogs can read! The
    letter *a* in psalm and calm when
pronounced with the sound of *a* in candle, is very notice-
    able, but

why should continents of misapprehension have to be ac-
    counted for by the
fact? Does it follow that because there are poisonous toad-
    stools
which resemble mushrooms, both are dangerous? In the case
    of mettlesomeness which may be
mistaken for appetite, of heat which may appear to be haste,
    no con-

clusions may be drawn. To have misapprehended the matter
    is to have confessed
that one has not looked far enough. The sublimated wisdom
of China, Egyptian discernment, the cataclysmic torrent of
    emotion compressed
in the verbs of the Hebrew language, the books of the man
    who is able

Poetry

I, too, dislike it: there are things that are important beyond all this
    fiddle.
  Reading it, however, with a perfect contempt for it, one discovers in
  it after all, a place for the genuine.
      Hands that can grasp, eyes
      that can dilate, hair that can rise
         if it must, these things are important not because a

high-sounding interpretation can be put upon them but because they
    are
  useful. When they become so derivative as to become unintelligible,
  the same thing may be said for all of us, that we
      do not admire what
      we cannot understand: the bat
         holding on upside down or in quest of something to

eat, elephants pushing, a wild horse taking a roll, a tireless wolf under
  a tree, the immovable critic twitching his skin like a horse that feels
  a flea, the base-
  ball fan, the statistician—
      nor is it valid
         to discriminate against 'business documents and

school-books'; all these phenomena are important. One must make a
    distinction
  however: when dragged into prominence by half poets, the result is
  not poetry,
  nor till the poets among us can be
      'literalists of
      the imagination'—above
         insolence and triviality and can present

for inspection, 'imaginary gardens with real toads in them', shall we
    have
  it. In the meantime, if you demand on the one hand,
  the raw material of poetry in
    all its rawness and

that which is on the other hand
    genuine, you are interested in poetry.

A Grave

Man looking into the sea,
taking the view from those who have as much right to it as
    you have to yourself,
it is human nature to stand in the middle of a thing,
but you cannot stand in the middle of this;
the sea has nothing to give but a well excavated grave.
The firs stand in a procession, each with an emerald turkey-
    foot at the top,
reserved as their contours, saying nothing;
repression, however, is not the most obvious characteristic
    of the sea;
the sea is a collector, quick to return a rapacious look.
There are others besides you who have worn that look–
whose expression is no longer a protest; the fish no longer
    investigate them
for their bones have not lasted:
men lower nets, unconscious of the fact that they are dese-
    crating a grave,
and row quickly away–the blades of the oars
moving together like the feet of water-spiders as if there
    were no such thing as death.
The wrinkles progress among themselves in a phalanx–
    beautiful under networks of foam,
and fade breathlessly while the sea rustles in and out of the
    seaweed;
the birds swim through the air at top speed, emitting cat-
    calls as heretofore–
the tortoise-shell scourges about the feet of the cliffs, in motion
    beneath them;
and the ocean, under the pulsation of lighthouses and noise
    of bell-buoys.

advances as usual, looking as if it were not that ocean in
    which dropped things are bound to sink–
in which if they turn and twist, it is neither with volition nor
    consciousness.

The Pangolin

Another armored animal–scale
    lapping scale with spruce-cone regularity until they
form the uninterrupted central
    tail-row! This near artichoke with head and legs and grit-equipped
      gizzard,
    the night miniature artist engineer is,
        yes, Leonardo da Vinci's replica–
            impressive animal and toiler of whom we seldom hear.
        Armor seems extra. But for him,
            the closing ear-ridge–
                or bare ear lacking even this small
                eminence and similarly safe

contracting nose and eye apertures
    impenetrably closable, are not; a true ant-eater,
not cockroach-eater, who endures
    exhausting solitary trips through unfamiliar ground at night,
    returning before sunrise; stepping in the moonlight,
        on the moonlight peculiarly, that the outside
            edges of his hands may bear the weight and save the claws
        for digging. Serpentined about
        the tree, he draws
            away from danger unpugnaciously,
            with no sound but a harmless hiss; keeping

the fragile grace of the Thomas-
    of-Leighton Buzzard Westminster Abbey wrought-iron vine, or
rolls himself into a ball that has
    power to defy all effort to unroll it; strongly intailed, neat
    head for core, on neck not breaking off, with curled-in feet.

Nevertheless he has sting-proof scales; and nest
   of rocks closed with earth from inside, which he can thus
     darken.
Sun and moon and day and night and man and beast
   each with a splendor
     which man in all his vileness cannot
     set aside; each with an excellence!

"Fearful yet to be feared," the armored
   ant-eater met by the driver-ant does not turn back, but
engulfs what he can, the flattened sword-
   edged leafpoints on the tail and artichoke set leg- and body-plates
   quivering violently when it retaliates
     and swarms on him. Compact like the furled fringed frill
     on the hat-brim of Gargallo's hollow iron head of a
   matador, he will drop and will
     then walk away
       unhurt, although if unintruded on,
       he cautiously works down the tree, helped

by his tail. The giant-pangolin-
   tail, graceful tool, as prop or hand or broom or ax, tipped like
an elephant's trunk with special skin,
   is not lost on this ant- and stone-swallowing uninjurable
   artichoke which simpletons thought a living fable
     whom the stones had nourished, whereas ants had done
     so. Pangolins are not aggressive animals; between
   dusk and day they have the not unchain-like machine-like
     form and frictionless creep of a thing
     made graceful by adversities, con-

versities. To explain grace requires
   a curious hand. If that which is at all were not forever,
why would those who graced the spires
   with animals and gathered there to rest, on cold luxurious
   low stone seats—a monk and monk and monk—between the thus
     ingenious roof supports, have slaved to confuse
     grace with a kindly manner, time in which to pay a debt,
   the cure for sins, a graceful use

of what are yet
    approved stone mullions branching out across
    the perpendiculars? A sailboat

was the first machine. Pangolins, made
    for moving quietly also, are models of exactness,
on four legs; on hind feet plantigrade,
    with certain postures of a man. Beneath sun and moon, man slaving
    to make his life more sweet, leaves half the flowers worth having,
        needing to choose wisely how to use his strength;
        a paper-maker like the wasp; a tractor of foodstuffs,
      like the ant; spidering a length
      of web from bluffs
        above a stream; in fighting, mechanicked
        like the pangolin; capsizing in

disheartenment. Bedizened or stark
    naked, man, the self, the being we call human, writing-
master to this world, griffons a dark
    "Like does not like like that is obnoxious"; and writes error with four
    r's. Among animals, *one* has a sense of humor.
        Humor saves a few steps, it saves years. Unignorant,
        modest and unemotional, and all emotion,
      he has everlasting vigor,
        power to grow,
        though there are few creatures who can make one
        breathe faster and make one erecter.

Not afraid of anything is he,
    and then goes cowering forth, tread paced to meet an obstacle
at every step. Consistent with the
    formula—warm blood, no gills, two pairs of hands and a few hairs—
        that
is a mammal; there he sits in his own habitat,
    serge-clad, strong-shod. The prey of fear, he, always
      curtailed, extinguished, thwarted by the dusk, work partly
      done,
      says to the alternating blaze,

"Again the sun!
anew each day; and new and new and new,
that comes into and steadies my soul."

What Are Years?

What is our innocence,
what is our guilt? All are
       naked, none is safe. And whence
is courage: the unanswered question,
the resolute doubt–
dumbly calling, deafly listening–that
is misfortune, even death,
       encourages others
       and in its defeat, stirs

       the soul to be strong? He
sees deep and is glad, who
       accedes to mortality
and in his imprisonment rises
upon himself as
the sea in a chasm, struggling to be
free and unable to be,
       in its surrendering
       finds its continuing.

So he who strongly feels,
behaves. The very bird,
       grown taller as he sings, steels
his form straight up. Though he is captive,
his mighty singing
says, satisfaction is a lowly
thing, how pure a thing is joy.
       This is mortality,
       this is eternity.

Spenser's Ireland

has not altered;–
   a place as kind as it is green,
   the greenest place I've never seen.
Every name is a tune.
Denunciations do not affect
      the culprit; nor blows, but it
is torture to him to not be spoken to.
They're natural,–
      the coat, like Venus'
mantle lined with stars,
buttoned close at the neck,–the sleeves new from disuse.

If in Ireland
   they play the harp backward at need,
   and gather at midday the seed
of the fern, eluding
their "giants all covered with iron," might
      there be fern seed for unlearn-
ing obduracy and for reinstating
the enchantment?
      Hindered characters
seldom have mothers
in Irish stories, but they all have grandmothers.

It was Irish;
   a match not a marriage was made
   when my great great grandmother'd said
with native genius for
disunion,"although your suitor be
      perfection, one objection
is enough; he is not
Irish." Outwitting
      the fairies, befriending the furies,
whoever again
and again says, "I'll never give in," never sees

that you're not free
   until you've been made captive by
   supreme belief,–credulity
you say? When large dainty
fingers tremblingly divide the wings
      of the fly for mid-July
with a needle and wrap it with peacock-tail,
or tie wool and
         buzzard's wing, their pride,
like the enchanter's
is in care, not madness. Concurring hands divide

flax for damask
   that when bleached by Irish weather
   has the silvered chamois-leather
water-tightness of a
skin. Twisted torcs and gold new-moon-shaped
      lunulae aren't jewelry
like the purple-coral fuchsia-tree's. Eire–
the guillemot
         so neat and the hen
of the heath and the
linnet spinet-sweet–bespeak relentlessness? Then

they are to me
   like enchanted Earl Gerald who
   changed himself into a stag, to
a great green-eyed cat of
the mountain. Discommodity makes
      them invisible; they've dis-
appeared. The Irish say your trouble is their
trouble and your
         joy their joy? I wish
I could believe it;
I am troubled, I'm dissatisfied, I'm Irish.

In Distrust of Merits

Strengthened to live, strengthened to die for
  medals and positioned victories?
They're fighting, fighting, fighting the blind
  man who thinks he sees,—
who cannot see that the enslaver is
enslaved; the hater, harmed. O shining O
    firm star, O tumultuous
      ocean lashed till small things go
    as they will, the mountainous
      wave makes us who look, know

depth. Lost at sea before they fought! O
  star of David, star of Bethlehem,
O black imperial lion
  of the Lord—emblem
of a risen world—be joined at last, be
joined. There is hate's crown beneath which all is
    death; there's love's without which none
      is king; the blessed deeds bless
    the halo. As contagion
      of sickness makes sickness,

contagion of trust can make trust. They're
  fighting in deserts and caves, one by
one, in battalions and squadrons;
  they're fighting that I
may yet recover from the disease, *my*
self; some have it lightly, some will die. "Man's
    wolf to man?" And we devour
      ourselves? The enemy could not
    have made a greater breach in our
    defenses. One pilot-

ing a blind man can escape him, but
  Job disheartened by false comfort knew,
that nothing is so defeating
  as a blind man who

can see. O alive who are dead, who are
proud not to see, O small dust of the earth
    that walks so arrogantly,
        trust begets power and faith is
    an affectionate thing. We
        vow, we make this promise

to the fighting–its's a promise–"We'll
    never hate black, white, red, yellow, Jew,
Gentile, Untouchable," We are
    not competent to
make our vows. With set jaw they are fighting,
fighting, fighting,–some we love whom we know,
    some we love but know not–that
        hearts may feel and not be numb.
    It cures me; or am I what
        I can't believe in? Some

in snow, some on crags, some in quicksands,
    little by little, much by much, they
are fighting fighting fighting that where
    there was death there may
be life. "When a man is prey to anger,
he is moved by outside things; when he holds
    his ground in patience patience
        patience, that is action or
    beauty," the soldier's defense
        and hardest armor for

the fight. The world's an orphan's home. Shall
    we never have peace without sorrow?
without pleas of the dying for
    help that won't come? O
quiet form upon the dust, I cannot
look and yet I must. If these great patient
    dyings–all these agonies
        and woundbearings and blood shed–
    can teach us how to live, these
        dyings were not wasted.

Hate-hardened heart, O heart of iron,
    iron is iron till it is rust.
There never was a war that was
    not inward; I must
fight till I have conquered in myself what
causes war, but I would not believe it.
    I inwardly did nothing.
      O Iscariotlike crime!
    Beauty is everlasting
      and dust is for a time.

T.S. ELIOT   [1888-1965]

Thomas Stearns Eliot was born in St. Louis, Missouri, to a prosperous and distinguished family. His father was a wealthy industrialist and his paternal grandfather a Unitarian minister who founded Washington University in 1859. He spent his summers in New England and attended the Milton Academy in Massachusetts before entering Harvard University in 1906. During these years, he was deeply influenced by George Santayana and Irving Babbitt, both of whom were on the Harvard Faculty. He completed his degree in only three years and then embarked upon graduate study in philosophy. After earning his master's degree in 1910, Eliot journeyed to Paris, where he studied for a year at the Sorbonne. He then returned to Harvard to begin a dissertation on the philosopher F.H. Bradley. Meanwhile, he pursued interests in a variety of other areas: social anthropology, French poetry, the Sanskrit and Pali languages, and Indic religion. During this time, he was also writing poetry of his own. In 1914, Eliot was awarded a travelling fellowship; he went to study at Marburg, Germany, but was forced to go to Oxford when World War I broke out. Then, in 1915, he decided against becoming a philosopher and an academic and, instead, chose to pursue a literary career. In the same year, he married Vivian Haigh-Wood after a brief courtship and resolved to settle permanently in England. His family was quite disappointed by this turn of events; his dissertation was finished and all that remained for him to receive a doctorate was to take his oral examination. They prevailed upon him to return to Harvard, and he booked to sail on a ship in April of 1916; however, the crossing was canceled due to the war and all thought of completing his degree thereupon ceased.

Eliot's earliest poems were rather undistinguished efforts written in the late-Romantic style. However, in 1908, through Arthur Symons' *The Symbolist Movement in Literature*, he was introduced to the French poet Jules Laforgue. Laforgue had rebelled against late-Romantic verse not by abandoning its stock themes, images, and attitudes but by exploiting them ironically. This approach and sensibility appealed to Eliot immensely. He went on to immerse himself in the whole of French symbolist and post-symbolist poetry, and this experience helped him arrive at a voice that was uniquely his own and uniquely modern. By 1911, his transformation had become evident in such poems as "Rhapsody on a Windy Night" and, especially, "The Love Song of J. Alfred Prufrock." In September of 1914, Eliot met Ezra Pound and showed him his work; Pound was deeply impressed. Despite Harriet Monroe's reservations, Pound prevailed upon her to print "Prufrock" in the June 1915 edition of her Chicago-based *Poetry* magazine. In 1917, Eliot's first book, *Prufrock and Other Observations,* appeared.

Subsequent to his marriage, Eliot taught grammar and secondary schools for two years but found the work intolerable. Thus, in 1917, he took work in the foreign department of Lloyd's Bank, a position at which he remained for eight years. While working for the bank, Eliot was in the habit of rising extremely early in order to write; he published many reviews and critical essays (which later gained great acclaim) and continued to write poetry. He began work on his great masterpiece, *The Waste Land*, around 1919 but was unable to complete it until 1921, when he was sent by a doctor to a Swiss sanitarium to recover from a nervous collapse. Upon his return, he gave Pound the manuscript, and Pound, in one of the most celebrated projects of editorship in literary history, helped prune the poem down to its present form. Published in 1922, *The Waste Land* stands as one of the great achievements in all of modern art. Stylistically, people likened its fragmented structure to cubist painting and compared its recurring images, themes, and symbols to the process of music. The poem offered its generation a chilling, unforgettable vision of the advancing decay of Western civilization. Eliot had clearly broken from traditional poetry, but it is interesting to observe how many of his contemporaries–poets who were dedicated to the development of a "new poetry"–were offended by *The Waste Land*. William Carlos Williams was particularly vocal in his opposition; he considered the work a "catastrophe" for modern American letters. Williams and those of a like mind were put off by the poem's learned allusions, its complex web of symbol and archetype, and its general difficulty. They considered it academic and anti-democratic. Doubtless, many of its critics were reacting out of their own intellectual insecurities; and, ultimately, their protestations could do little to obscure the merits of *The Waste Land*. Pound called it "the justification of our modern experiment, since 1900." The poem won the Dial Award for 1922 and stands as the signal event of the high Modernist period.

In the same year, Eliot founded *The Criterion*, a cultural magazine he was to edit for seventeen years. In 1927, Eliot was granted British citizenship and was confirmed in the Anglican Church; by this time, he had left Lloyd's bank for an editing position at Faber and Faber. He became interested in writing for the theatre and, in the following decades, produced verse dramas such as *Murder in the Cathedral* (1935), *The Family Reunion* (1939), *The Cocktail Party* (1949), and *The Confidence Man* (1953). In 1943, he published his late poetic masterpiece, *Four Quartets*, a group of poems exploring religious and philosophic themes. Even more than *The Waste Land*, these poems are structurally akin to music (modelled, some suggest, on Beethoven's late quartets). Eliot was awarded the Order of Merit by the British Crown in 1948 and, that same year, received the Nobel Prize for literature.

The Love Song of J. Alfred Prufrock

S'io credessi che mia risposta fosse
a persona che mai tornasse al mondo,
questa fiamma staria senza più scosse.
Ma per ciò che giammai di questo fondo
non tornò vivo alcun, s'i'odo il vero,
senza tema d'infamia ti rispondo.

Let us go then, you and I,
When the evening is spread out against the sky
Like a patient etherised upon a table;
Let us go, through certain half-deserted streets,
The muttering retreats
Of restless nights in one-night cheap hotels
And sawdust restaurants with oyster-shells:
Streets that follow like a tedious argument
Of insidious intent
To lead you to an overwhelming question . . .
Oh, do not ask, 'What is it?'
Let us go and make our visit.

In the room the women come and go
Talking of Michelangelo.

The yellow fog that rubs its back upon the window-panes,
The yellow smoke that rubs its muzzle on the window-panes,
Licked its tongue into the corners of the evening,
Lingered upon the pools that stand in drains,
Let fall upon its back the soot that falls from chimneys,
Slipped by the terrace, made a sudden leap,
And seeing that it was a soft October night,
Curled once about the house, and fell asleep.

And indeed there will be time
For the yellow smoke that slides along the street
Rubbing its back upon the window-panes;
There will be time, there will be time
To prepare a face to meet the faces that you meet;

There will be time to murder and create,
And time for all the works and days of hands
That lift and drop a question on your plate;
Time for you and time for me,
And time yet for a hundred indecisions,
And for a hundred visions and revisions,
Before the taking of a toast and tea.

In the room the women come and go
Talking of Michelangelo.

And indeed there will be time
To wonder, 'Do I dare?' and, 'Do I dare?'
Time to turn back and descend the stair,
With a bald spot in the middle of my hair–
(They will say: 'How his hair is growing thin!')
My morning coat, my collar mounting firmly to the chin,
My necktie rich and modest, but asserted by a simple pin–
(They will say: 'But how his arms and legs are thin!')
Do I dare
Disturb the universe?
In a minute there is time
For decisions and revisions which a minute will reverse.

For I have known them all already, known them all–
Have known the evenings, mornings, afternoons,
I have measured out my life with coffee spoons;
I know the voices dying with a dying fall
Beneath the music from a farther room.
      So how should I presume?

And I have known the eyes already, known them all–
The eyes that fix you in a formulated phrase,
And when I am formulated, sprawling on a pin,
When I am pinned and wriggling on the wall,
Then how should I begin
To spit out all the butt-ends of my days and ways?
      And how should I presume?

And I have known the arms already, known them all—
Arms that are braceleted and white and bare
(But in the lamplight, downed with light brown hair!)
Is it perfume from a dress
That makes me so digress?
Arms that lie along a table, or wrap about a shawl.
    And should I then presume?
    And how should I begin?

     · · · · ·

Shall I say, I have gone at dusk through narrow streets
And watched the smoke that rises from the pipes
Of lonely men in shirt-sleeves, leaning out of windows? . . .

I should have been a pair of ragged claws
Scuttling across the floors of silent seas.

     · · · · ·

And the afternoon, the evening, sleeps so peacefully!
Smoothed by long fingers,
Asleep . . . tired . . . or it malingers,
Stretched on the floor, here beside you and me.
Should I, after tea and cakes and ices,
Have the strength to force the moment to its crisis?
But though I have wept and fasted, wept and prayed,
Though I have seen my head (grown slightly bald) brought in
    upon a platter,
I am no prophet—and here's no great matter;
I have seen the moment of my greatness flicker,
And I have seen the eternal Footman hold my coat, and snicker,
And in short, I was afraid.

And would it have been worth it, after all,
After the cups, the marmalade, the tea,
Among the porcelain, among some talk of you and me,
Would it have been worth while,
To have bitten off the matter with a smile,
To have squeezed the universe into a ball
To roll it towards some overwhelming question,

To say: 'I am Lazarus, come from the dead,
Come back to tell you all, I shall tell you all'–
If one, settling a pillow by her head,
   Should say: 'That is not what I meant at all.
   That is not it, at all.'

And would it have been worth it, after all,
Would it have been worth while,
After the sunsets and the dooryards and the sprinkled streets,
After the novels, after the teacups, after the skirts that trail along
   the floor–
And this, and so much more?–
It is impossible to say just what I mean!
But as if a magic lantern threw the nerves in patterns on a
   screen:
Would it have been worth while

If one, settling a pillow or throwing off a shawl,
And turning toward the window, should say:
   'That is not it at all,
That is not what I meant, at all.'
   . . . . .

No! I am not Prince Hamlet, nor was meant to be;
Am an attendant lord, one that will do
To swell a progress, start a scene or two,
Advise the prince; no doubt, an easy tool
Deferential, glad to be of use,
Politic, cautious, and meticulous;
Full of high sentence, but a bit obtuse;
At times, indeed, almost ridiculous–
Almost, at times, the Fool.

I grow old . . . I grow old . . .
I shall wear the bottoms of my trousers rolled.

Shall I part my hair behind? Do I dare to eat a peach?
I shall wear white flannel trousers, and walk upon the beach.
I have heard the mermaids singing, each to each.

I do not think that they will sing to me.

I have seen them riding seaward on the waves
Combing the white hair of the waves blown back
When the wind blows the water white and black.

We have lingered in the chambers of the sea
By sea-girls wreathed with seaweed red and brown
Till human voices wake us, and we drown.

Rhapsody on a Windy Night

Twelve o'clock.
Along the reaches of the street
Held in a lunar synthesis,
Whispering lunar incantations
Dissolve the floors of memory
And all its clear relations,
Its divisions and precisions.
Every street lamp that I pass
Beats like a fatalistic drum,
And through the spaces of the dark
Midnight shakes the memory
As a madman shakes a dead geranium.

Half-past one,
The street-lamp sputtered,
The street-lamp muttered,
The street-lamp said, 'Regard that woman
Who hesitates toward you in the light of the door
Which opens on her like a grin.
You see the border of her dress
Is torn and stained with sand,
And you see the corner of her eye
Twists like a crooked pin.'

The memory throws up high and dry
A crowd of twisted things;
A twisted branch upon the beach
Eaten smooth, and polished
As if the world gave up
The secret of its skeleton,
Stiff and white.
A broken spring in a factory yard,
Rust that clings to the form that the strength has left
Hard and curled and ready to snap.

Half-past two,
The street-lamp said,
'Remark the cat which flattens itself in the gutter,
Slips out its tongue
And devours a morsel of rancid butter.'
So the hand of the child, automatic,
Slipped out and pocketed a toy that was running along the quay.
I could see nothing behind that child's eye.
I have seen eyes in the street
Trying to peer through lighted shutters,
And a crab one afternoon in a pool,
And old crab with barnacles on his back,
Gripped the end of a stick which I held him.

Half-past three,
The lamp sputtered,
The lamp muttered in the dark.
The lamp hummed:
'Regard the moon,
La lune ne garde aucune rancune,
She winks a feeble eye,
She smiles into corners.
(She smooths the hair of the grass.)
The moon has lost her memory.
A washed-out smallpox cracks her face,
Her hand twists a paper rose,

That smells of dust and eau de Cologne,
She is alone
With all the old nocturnal smells
That cross and cross across her brain.'
The reminiscence comes
Of sunless dry geraniums
And dust in crevices,
Smells of chestnuts in the streets,
And female smells in shuttered rooms,
And cigarettes in corridors
And cocktail smells in bars.

The lamp said,
'Four o'clock,
Here is the number on the door.
Memory!
You have the key,
The little lamp spreads a ring on the stair.
Mount.
The bed is open; the tooth-brush hangs on the wall,
Put your shoes at the door, sleep, prepare for life.'

The last twist of the knife.

The Waste Land

'Nam Sibyllam quidem Cumis ego ipse oculis meis vidi in ampulla
pendere, et cum illi pueri dicerent: Ειβυλλα τι Θελεις; respondebat illa:
αποθανειν Θελως'

For Ezra Pound
il miglior fabbro.

I. The Burial of the Dead

April is the cruellest month, breeding
Lilacs out of the dead land, mixing

Memory and desire, stirring
Dull roots with spring rain.
Winter kept us warm, covering
Earth in forgetful snow, feeding
A little life with dried tubers.
Summer surprised us, coming over the Starnbergersee
With a shower of rain; we stopped in the colonnade,
And went on in sunlight, into the Hofgarten,
And drank coffee, and talked for an hour.
Bin gar keine Russin, stamm' aus Litauen, echt deutsch.
And when we were children, staying at the arch-duke's,
My cousin's, he took me out on a sled,
And I was frightened. He said, Marie,
Marie, hold on tight. And down we went.
In the mountains, there you feel free.
I read, much of the night, and go south in the winter.

What are the roots that clutch, what branches grow
Out of this stony rubbish? Son of man,
You cannot say, or guess, for you know only
A heap of broken images, where the sun beats,
And the dead tree gives no shelter, the cricket no relief,
And the dry stone no sound of water. Only
There is shadow under this red rock,
(Come in under the shadow of this red rock),
And I will show you something different from either
Your shadow at morning striding behind you
Or your shadow at evening rising to meet you;
I will show you fear in a handful of dust.
        Frisch weht der Wind
        Der Heimat zu
        Mein Irisch Kind,
        Wo weilest du?
'You gave me hyacinths first a year ago;
They called me the hyacinth girl.'
–Yet when we came back, late, from the hyacinth garden,
Your arms full, and your hair wet, I could not
Speak, and my eyes failed, I was neither
Living nor dead, and I knew nothing,

Looking into the heart of light, the silence.
Oed' und leer das Meer.

Madame Sosostris, famous clairvoyante,
Had a bad cold, nevertheless
Is known to be the wisest woman in Europe,
With a wicked pack of cards. Here, said she,
Is your card, the drowned Phoenician Sailor,
(Those are pearls that were his eyes. Look!)
Here is Belladonna, the Lady of the Rocks,
The lady of situations.
Here is the man with three staves, and here the Wheel,
And here is the one-eyed merchant, and this card,
Which is blank, is something he carries on his back,
Which I am forbidden to see. I do not find
The Hanged Man. Fear death by water.
I see crowds of people, walking round in a ring.
Thank you. If you see dear Mrs. Equitone,
Tell her I bring the horoscope myself:
One must be so careful these days.
Unreal City,
Under the brown fog of a winter dawn,
A crowd flowed over London Bridge, so many,
I had not thought death had undone so many.
Sighs, short and infrequent, were exhaled,
And each man fixed his eyes before his feet.
Flowed up the hill and down King William Street,
To where Saint Mary Woolnoth kept the hours
With a dead sound on the final stroke of nine.
There I saw one I knew, and stopped him, crying: 'Stetson!
'You who were with me in the ships at Mylae!
'That corpse you planted last year in your garden,
'Has it begun to sprout? Will it bloom this year?
'Or has the sudden frost disturbed its bed?
'O keep the Dog far hence, that's friend to men,
'Or with his nails he'll dig it up again!
'You! hypocrite lecteur!-mom semblable,-mon frére!'

II. A Game of Chess

The Chair she sat in, like a burnished throne,
Glowed on the marble, where the glass
Held up by standards wrought with fruited vines
From which a golden Cupidon peeped out
(Another hid his eyes behind his wing)
Doubled the flames of sevenbranched candelabra
Reflecting light upon the table as
The glitter of her jewels rose to meet it,
From satin cases poured in rich profusion.
In vials of ivory and coloured glass
Unstoppered, lurked her strange synthetic perfumes,
Unguent, powdered, or liquid–troubled, confused
And drowned the sense in odours; stirred by the air
That freshened from the window, these ascended
In fattening the prolonged candle-flames,
Flung their smoke into the laquearia,
Stirring the pattern on the coffered ceiling.
Huge sea-wood fed with copper
Burned green and orange, framed by the coloured stone,
In which sad light a carvèd dolphin swam.
Above the antique mantel was displayed
As though a window gave upon the sylvan scene
The change of Philomel, by the barbarous king
So rudely forced; yet there the nightingale
Filled all the desert with inviolable voice
And still she cried, and still the world pursues,
'Jug Jug' to dirty ears.
And other withered stumps of time
Were told upon the walls; staring forms
Leaned out, leaning, hushing the room enclosed.

Footsteps shuffled on the stair.
Under the firelight, under the brush, her hair
Spread out in fiery points
Glowed into words, then would be savagely still.

'My nerves are bad to-night. Yes, bad. Stay with me.
'Speak to me. Why do you never speak. Speak.
     'What are you thinking of? What thinking? What?
'I never know what you are thinking. Think.'

I think we are in rats' alley
Where the dead men lost their bones.

'What is that noise?'
                    The wind under the door.
'What is that noise now? What is the wind doing?'
                    Nothing again nothing.
                                              'Do
'You know nothing? Do you see nothing? Do you remember
'Nothing?'

     I remember
Those are pearls that were his eyes.
'Are you alive, or not? Is there nothing in your head?'
                                                      But
O O O O that Shakespeherian Rag—
It's so elegant
So intelligent
'What shall I do now? What shall I do?'
'I shall rush out as I am, and walk the street
'With my hair down, so. What shall we do tomorrow?
'What shall we ever do?'
                    The hot water at ten.
And if it rains, a closed car at four.
And we shall play a game of chess,
Pressing lidless eyes and waiting for a knock upon the door.

When Lil's husband got demobbed, I said—
I didn't mince my words, I said to her myself,
Hurry up please its time
Now Albert's coming back, make yourself a bit smart.
He'll want to know what you done with that money he gave
     you
To get yourself some teeth. He did, I was there.

You have them all out, Lil, and get a nice set,
He said, I swear, I can't bear to look at you.
And no more can't I, I said, and think of poor Albert,
He's been in the army four years, he wants a good time,
And if you don't give it him, there's others will, I said.
Oh is there, she said. Something o' that, I said.
Then I'll know who to thank, she said, and give me a straight
    look.
Hurry up please its time
If you don't like it you can get on with it, I said.
Others can pick and choose if you can't.
But if Albert makes off, it won't be for lack of telling.
You ought to be ashamed, I said, to look so antique.
(And her only thirty-one.)
I can't help it, she said, pulling a long face,
It's them pills I took, to bring it off, she said.
(She's had five already, and nearly died of young George.)
The chemist said it would be all right, but I've never been
    the same.
You *are* a proper fool, I said.
Well, if Albert won't leave you alone, there it is, I said,
What you get married for if you don't want children?
Hurry up please its time
Well, that Sunday Albert was home, they had a hot gammon,
And they asked me in to dinner, to get the beauty of it hot–
Hurry up please its time
Hurry up please its time
Goonight Bill. Goonight Lou. Goonight May. Goonight.
Ta ta. Goonight. Goonight.
Good night, ladies, good night, sweet ladies, good night,
    good night.

III. The Fire Sermon

The river's tent is broken; the last fingers of leaf
Clutch and sink into the wet bank. The wind
Crosses the brown land, unheard. The nymphs are departed.

Sweet Thames, run softly, till I end my song.
The river bears no empty bottles, sandwich papers,
Silk handkerchiefs, cardboard boxes, cigarette ends
Or other testimony of summer nights. The nymphs are
        departed.
And their friends, the loitering heirs of City directors;
Departed, have left no addresses.
By the waters of Leman I sat down and wept . . .
Sweet Thames, run softly till I end my song,
Sweet Thames, run softly, for I speak not loud or long.
But at my back in a cold blast I hear
The rattle of the bones, and chuckle spread from ear to ear.

A rat crept softly through the vegetation
Dragging its slimy belly on the bank
While I was fishing in the dull canal
On a winter evening round behind the gashouse
Musing upon the king my brother's wreck
And on the king my father's death before him.
White bodies naked on the low damp ground
And bones cast in a little low dry garret,
Rattled by the rat's foot only, year to year.
But at my back from time to time I hear
The sound of horns and motors, which shall bring
Sweeney to Mrs. Porter in the spring.
O the moon shone bright on Mrs. Porter
And on her daughter
They wash their feet in soda water
Et O ces voix d'enfants, chantant dans la coupole!

Twit twit twit
Jug jug jug jug jug jug
So rudely forc'd.
Tereu

Unreal City
Under the brown fog of a winter noon
Mr. Eugenides, the Smyrna merchant
Unshaven, with a pocket full of currants

C.i.f. London: documents at sight,
Asked me in demotic French
To luncheon at the Cannon Street Hotel
Followed by a weekend at the Metropole.

At the violet hour, when the eyes and back
Turn upward from the desk, when the human engine waits
Like a taxi throbbing waiting,
I Tiresias, though blind, throbbing between two lives,
Old man with wrinkled female breasts, can see
At the violet hour, the evening hour that strives
Homeward, and brings the sailor home from sea,
The typist home at teatime, clears her breakfast, lights
Her stove, and lays out food in tins.
Out of the window perilously spread
Her drying combinations touched by the sun's last rays,
On the divan are piled (at night her bed)
Stockings, slippers, camisoles, and stays.
I Tiresias, old man with wrinkled dugs
Perceived the scene, and foretold the rest—

I too awaited the expected guest.
He, the young man carbuncular, arrives,
A small house agent's clerk, with one bold stare,
One of the low on whom assurance sits
As a silk hat on a Bradford millionaire.
The time is now propitious, as he guesses,
The meal is ended, she is bored and tired,
Endeavours to engage her in caresses
Which still are unreproved, if undesired.
Flushed and decided, he assaults at once;
Exploring hands encounter no defence;
His vanity requires no response,
And makes a welcome of indifference.
(And I Tiresias have foresuffered all
Enacted on this same divan or bed;
I who have sat by Thebes below the wall
And walked among the lowest of the dead.)
            Bestows one final patronising kiss,

And gropes his way, finding the stairs unlit . . .

She turns and looks a moment in the glass,
Hardly aware of her departed lover;
Her brain allows one half-formed thought to pass:
'Well now that's done: and I'm glad it's over.'
When lovely woman stoops to folly and
Paces about her room again, alone,
She smoothes her hair with automatic hand,
And puts a record on the gramophone.

'This music crept by me upon the waters'
And along the Strand, up Queen Victoria Street.
O City city, I can sometimes hear
Beside a public bar in Lower Thames Street,
The pleasant whining of a mandoline
And a clatter and a chatter from within
Where fishmen lounge at noon: where the walls
Of Magnus Martyr hold
Inexplicable splendour of Ionian white and gold.

      The river sweats
      Oil and tar
      The barges drift
      With the turning tide
      Red sails
      Wide
      To leeward, swing on the heavy spar.
      The barges wash
      Drifting logs
      Down Greenwich reach
      Past the Isle of Dogs.
            Weialala leia
            Wallala leialala

      Elizabeth and Leicester
      Beating oars
      The stern was formed

A gilded shell
Red and gold
The brisk swell
Rippled both shores
Southwest wind
Carried down stream
The peal of bells
White towers
      Weialala leia
      Wallala leialala

'Trams and dusty trees.
Highbury bore me. Richmond and Kew
Undid me. By Richmond I raised my knees
Supine on the floor of a narrow canoe.'

'My feet are at Moorgate, and my heart
Under my feet. After the event
He wept. He promised "a new start."
I made no comment. What should I resent?'

'On Margate Sands.
I can connect
Nothing with nothing.
The broken fingernails of dirty hands.
My people humble people who expect
Nothing.'
      la la

To Carthage then I came

Burning burning burning burning
O Lord Thou pluckest me out
O Lord Thou pluckest

burning

IV. Death by Water

Phlebas the Phoenician, a fortnight dead,
Forgot the cry of gulls, and the deep sea swell
And the profit and loss.
                              A current under sea
Picked his bones in whispers. As he rose and fell
He passed the stages of his age and youth
Entering the whirlpool.
                              Gentile or Jew
O you who turn the wheel and look to windward,
Consider Phlebas, who was once handsome and tall as you.

V. What the Thunder Said

After the torchlight red on sweaty faces
After the frosty silence in the gardens
After the agony in stony places
The shouting and the crying
Prison and palace and reverberation
Of thunder of spring over distant mountains
He who was living is now dead
We who were living are now dying
With a little patience

Here is no water but only rock
Rock and no water and the sandy road
The road winding above among the mountains
Which are mountains of rock without water
If there were water we should stop and drink
Amongst the rock one cannot stop or think
Sweat is dry and feet are in the sand
If there were only water amongst the rock
Dead mountain mouth of carious teeth that cannot spit
Here one can neither stand nor lie nor sit
There is not even silence in the mountains
But dry sterile thunder without rain

There is not even solitude in the mountains
But red sullen faces sneer and snarl
From doors of mudcracked houses
                                        If there were water
        And no rock
        If there were rock
        And also water
        And water
        A spring
        A pool among the rock
        If there were the sound of water only
        Not the cicada
        And dry grass singing
        But sound of water over a rock
        Where the hermit-thrush sings in the pine trees
        Drip drop drip drop drop drop drop
        But there is no water

Who is the third who walks always beside you?
When I count, there are only you and I together
But when I look ahead up the white road
There is always another one walking beside you
Gliding wrapt in a brown mantle, hooded
I do not know whether a man or a woman
–But who is that on the other side of you?

What is that sound high in the air
Murmur of maternal lamentation
Who are those hooded hordes swarming
Over endless plains, stumbling in cracked earth
Ringed by the flat horizon only
What is the city over the mountains
Cracks and reforms and bursts in the violet air
Falling towers
Jerusalem Athens Alexandria
Vienna London
Unreal

A woman drew her long black hair out tight
And fiddled whisper music on those strings
And bats with baby faces in the violet light
Whistled, and beat their wings
And crawled head downward down a blackened wall
And upside down in air were towers
Tolling reminiscent bells, that kept the hours
And voices singing out of empty cisterns and exhausted wells

In this decayed hole among the mountains
In the faint moonlight, the grass is singing
Over the tumbled graves, about the chapel
There is the empty chapel, only the wind's home.
It has no windows, and the door swings,
Dry bones can harm no one.
Only a cock stood on the rooftree
Co co rico co co rico
In a flash of lightning. Then a damp gust
Bringing rain

Ganga was sunken, and the limp leaves
Waited for rain, while the black clouds
Gathered far distant, over Himavant.
The jungle crouched, humped in silence.
Then spoke the thunder
Da
Datta: what have we given?
My friend, blood shaking my heart
The awful daring of a moment's surrender
Which an age of prudence can never retract
By this, and this only, we have existed
Which is not to be found in our obituaries
Or in memories draped by the beneficent spider
Or under seals broken by the lean solicitor
In our empty rooms
Da
Dayadhvam: I have heard the key
Turn in the door once and turn once only
We think of the key, each in his prison

Thinking of the key, each confirms a prison
Only at nightfall, aethereal rumours
Revive for a moment a broken Coriolanus
Da
*Damyata:*The boat responded
Gaily, to the hand expert with sail and oar
The sea was calm, your heart would have responded
Gaily, when invited, beating obedient
To controlling hands

                         I sat upon the shore
Fishing, with the arid plain behind me
Shall I at least set my lands in order?
London Bridge is falling down falling down falling down
Poi s'ascose nel foco che gli affina
Quando fiam uti chelidon–O swallow swallow
Le Prince d'Aquitaine à la tour abolie
These fragments I have shored against my ruins
Why then Ile fit you. Hieronymo's mad againe.
Datta. Dayadhvam. Damyata.
                 Shantih   shantih   shantih

The Hollow Men

A penny for the Old Guy

I

We are the hollow men
We are the stuffed men
Leaning together
Headpiece filled with straw. Alas!
Our dried voices, when
We whisper together
Are quiet and meaningless
As wind in dry grass

Or rats' feet over broken glass
In our dry cellar

Shape without form, shade without colour,
Paralysed force, gesture without motion;

Those who have crossed
With direct eyes, to death's other Kingdom
Remember us–if at all–not as lost
Violent souls, but only
As the hollow men
The stuffed men.

II

Eyes I dare not meet in dreams
In death's dream kingdom
These do not appear:
There, the eyes are
Sunlight on a broken column
There, is a tree swinging
And voices are
In the wind's singing
More distant and more solemn
Than a fading star.

Let me be no nearer
In death's dream kingdom
Let me also wear
Such deliberate disguises
Rat's coat, crowskin, crossed staves
In a field
Behaving as the wind behaves
No nearer–

Not that final meeting
In the twilight kingdom

III

This is the dead land
This is cactus land
Here the stone images
Are raised, here they receive
The supplication of a dead man's hand
Under the twinkle of a fading star.

Is it like this
In death's other kingdom
Waking alone
At the hour when we are
Trembling with tenderness
Lips that would kiss
Form prayers to broken stone.

IV

The eyes are not here
There are no eyes here
In this valley of dying stars
In this hollow valley
This broken jaw of our lost kingdoms

In this last of meeting places
We grope together
And avoid speech
Gathered on this beach of the tumid river

Sightless, unless
The eyes reappear
As the perpetual star
Multifoliate rose
Of death's twilight kingdom
The hope only
Of empty men.

V

Here we go round the prickly pear
Prickly pear prickly pear
Here we go round the prickly pear
At five o'clock in the morning.

Between the idea
And the reality
Between the motion
And the act
Falls the Shadow

                                        For Thine is the Kingdom

Between the conception
And the creation
Between the emotion
And the response
Falls the Shadow

                                        Life is very long

Between the desire
And the spasm
Between the potency
And the existence
Between the essence
And the descent
Falls the Shadow

                                        For Thine is the Kingdom

For Thine is
Life is
For Thine is the

This is the way the world ends
This is the way the world ends
This is the way the world ends
Not with a bang but a whimper.

Four Quartets, Selections

Burnt Norton

τον λογον δ]εοντο, ξυνου ζωυσιν οι πολλοι
ω, ιδιαν εχοντε, φρονησιν.
                          I. p. 77. Fr. 2.
οδο, ανω κατω μια και ωυτη
                          I. p. 89. Fr. 60.
              Diels: *Die Fragmente der Vorsokratiker (Herakleitus)*

I

Time present and time past
Are both perhaps present in time future,
And time future contained in time past.
If all time is eternally present
All time is unredeemable.
What might have been is an abstraction
Remaining a perpetual possibility
Only in a world of speculation.
What might have been and what has been
Point to one end, which is always present.
Footfalls echo in the memory
Down the passage which we did not take
Towards the door we never opened
Into the rose-garden. My words echo
Thus, in your mind.
                          But to what purpose
Disturbing the dust on a bowl of rose-leaves
I do not know.
                          Other echoes
Inhabit the garden. Shall we follow?
Quick, said the bird, find them, find them,
Round the corner. Through the first gate,
Into our first world, shall we follow
The deception of the thrush? Into our first world.
There they were, dignified, invisible,

Moving without pressure, over the dead leaves,
In the autumn heat, through the vibrant air,
And the bird called, in response to
The unheard music hidden in the shrubbery,
And the unseen eyebeam crossed, for the roses
Had the look of flowers that are looked at.
There they were as our guests, accepted and accepting.
So we moved, and they, in a formal pattern,
Along the empty alley, into the box circle,
To look down into the drained pool.
Dry the pool, dry concrete, brown edged,
And the pool was filled with water out of sunlight,
And the lotos rose, quietly, quietly,
The surface glittered out of heart of light,
And they were behind us, reflected in the pool.
Then a cloud passed, and the pool was empty.
Go, said the bird, for the leaves were full of children,
Hidden excitedly, containing laughter.
Go, go, go, said the bird: human kind
Cannot bear very much reality.
Time past and time future
What might have been and what has been
Point to one end, which is always present.

II

Garlic and sapphires in the mud
Clot the bedded axle-tree
The trilling wire in the blood
Sings below inveterate scars
Appeasing long forgotten wars.
The dance along the artery
The circulation of the lymph
Are figured in the drift of stars
Ascend to summer in the tree
We move above the moving tree
In light upon the figured leaf
And hear upon the sodden floor
Below, the boarhound and the boar

Pursue their pattern as before
But reconciled among the stars.

At the still point of the turning world. Neither flesh nor
    fleshless;
Neither from nor towards; at the still point, there the
    is,
But neither arrest nor movement. And do not call it fixity,
Where past and future are gathered. Neither movement from
    nor towards,
Neither ascent nor decline. Except for the point, the
    still point,
There would be no dance, and there is only the dance.
I can only say, *there* we have been: but I cannot say where
And I cannot say, how long, for that is to place it in time.

The inner freedom from the practical desire,
The release from action and suffering, release from
    inner
And the outer compulsion, yet surrounded
By a grace of sense, a white light still and moving,
Erhebung without motion, concentration
Without elimination, both a new world
And the old made explicit, understood
In the completion of its partial ecstasy,
The resolution of its partial horror.
Yet the enchainment of past and future
Woven in the weakness of the changing body,
Protects mankind from heaven and damnation
Which flesh cannot endure.
                        Time past and time future
Allow but a little consciousness.
To be conscious is not to be in time
But only in time can the moment in the rose-garden,
The moment in the arbour where the rain beat,
The moment in the draughty church at smokefall
Be remembered; involved with past and future.
Only through time time is conquered.

III

Here is a place of disaffection
Time before and time after
In a dim light: neither daylight
Investing form with lucid stillness
Turning shadow into transient beauty
With slow rotation suggestion permanence
Nor darkness to purify the soul
Emptying the sensual with deprivation
Cleansing affection from the temporal.
Neither plenitude nor vacancy. Only a flicker
Over the strained time-ridden faces
Distracted from distraction by distraction
Filled with fancies and empty of meaning
Tumid apathy with no concentration
Men and bits of paper, whirled by the cold wind
That blows before and after time,
Wind in and out of unwholesome lungs
Time before and time after.
Eructation of unhealthy souls
Into the faded air, the torpid
Driven on the wind that sweeps the gloomy hills of London,
Hampstead and Clerkenwell, Campden and Putney,
Highgate, Primrose and Ludgate. Not here
Not here the darkness, in this twittering world.

Descend lower, descend only
Into the world of perpetual solitude,
World not world, but that which is not world,
Internal darkness, deprivation
And destitution of all property,
Desiccation of the world of sense,
Evacuation of the world of fancy,
Inoperancy of the world of spirit;
This is the one way, and the other
Is the same, not in movement
But abstention from movement; while the world moves

In appetency, on its metalled ways
Of time past and time future.

IV

Time and the bell have buried the day,
The black cloud carries the sun away.
Will the sunflower turn to us, will the clematis
Stray down, bend to us; tendril and spray
Clutch and cling?
Chill
Fingers of yew be curled
Down on us? After the kingfisher's wing
Has answered light to light, and is silent, the light is still
At the still point of the turning world.

V

Words move, music moves
Only in time; but that which is only living
Can only die. Words, after speech, reach
Into the silence. (Only by the form, the pattern,
Can words or music reach
The stillness, as a Chinese jar still
Moves perpetually in its stillness.)
Not the stillness of the violin, while the note lasts,
Not that only, but the co-existence,
Or say that the end precedes the beginning,
And the end and the beginning were always there
Before the beginning and after the end.
And all is always now. Words strain,
Crack and sometimes break, under the burden,
Under the tension, slip, slide, perish,
Decay with imprecision, will not stay in place,
Will not stay still. Shrieking voices
Scolding, mocking, or merely chattering,
Always assail them. The Word in the desert
Is most attacked by voices of temptation,

The crying shadow in the funeral dance,
The loud lament of the disconsolate chimera.
The detail of the pattern is movement,
As in the figure of the ten stairs.
Desire itself is movement
Not in itself desirable;
Love is itself unmoving,
Only the cause and end of movement,
Timeless, and undesiring
Except in the aspect of time
Caught in the form of limitation
Between un-being and being.
Sudden in a shaft of sunlight
Even while the dust moves
There rises the hidden laughter
Of children in the foliage
Quick now, here, now, always—
Ridiculous the waste sad time
Stretching before and after.

JOHN CROWE RANSOM   [1888-1974]

The son of a Methodist minister, John Crowe Ransom was born in Pulaski, Tennessee. He studied philosophy and the classics at Vanderbilt University, where he received a B.A. in 1909. He continued his studies at Oxford University as a Rhodes Scholar, earning another B.A. in 1913. In the following year, he began teaching English literature at Vanderbilt but left when World War I broke out to serve in the artillery. Afterwards, he resumed his studies at France's Grenoble University, and it was during this time that his first book of verse, *Poems Without God* (1919) was published. He soon returned to Vanderbilt, where he became the center of a group that came to be known as the Fugitives. Comprised of such figures as Allen Tate, Robert Penn Warren, and Donald Davidson, the Fugitives met fortnightly to discuss philosophy and to read one another their poetry. Between 1922 and 1925, the group published the influential journal *The Fugitive*. Some of Ransom's most distinguished verse first appeared in this publication. In 1937, Ransom moved to Kenyon College in Ohio, where he was appointed the Carnegie Professor of Poetry. Two years later, he founded another important journal, the *Kenyon Review*, which he edited until his retirement in 1959.

Ransom is widely considered to be the finest Southern poet of his generation. While his verse celebrates traditional Southern values, it eschews sentimentality and is characterized by wit and intellectual sophistication. For Ransom, the North, with its emphasis on technology and industrialism, epitomized all that was wrong with modern culture. He felt that the modern mindset, prone to intellectual abstraction, was ultimately vacant; Ransom preferred the calmer ways of the South: close community and family ties, a well-defined social structure, time-worn Protestant religious values, and the beauties of the rural landscape. This, he felt, was the environment to which the human psyche was best suited.

By the time Ransom reached his forties, he was concentrating more on literary criticism than on verse. *The New Criticism* (1941) is indeed one of the key works of American literary theory. As opposed to previous critical methodologies, which were concerned with philosophic, historic or biographical contexts of literary works, "New Criticism" called for

close—indeed exclusive—attention to the text itself. In the years follow-
ing the second World War, this methodology dominated both literary
scholarship and teaching.

Dead Boy

The little cousin is dead, by foul subtraction,
A green bough from Virginia's aged tree,
And none of the county kin like the transaction,
Nor some of the world of outer dark, like me.

A boy not beautiful, nor good, nor clever,
A black cloud full of storms too hot for keeping,
A sword beneath his mother's heart–yet never
Woman bewept her babe as this is weeping.

A pig with a pasty face, so I had said,
Squealing for cookies, kinned by poor pretense
With a noble house. But the little man quite dead,
I see the forebears' antique lineaments.

The elder men have strode by the box of death
To the wide flag porch, and muttering low send round
The bruit of the day. O friendly waste of breath!
Their hearts are hurt with a deep dynastic wound.

He was pale and little, the foolish neighbors say;
The first-fruits, saith the Preacher, the Lord hath taken;
But this was the old tree's late branch wrenched away,
Grieving the sapless limbs, the shorn and shaken.

Bells for John Whiteside's Daughter

There was such speed in her little body,
And such lightness in her footfall,
It is no wonder that her brown study
Astonishes us all.

Her wars were bruited in our high window.
We looked among orchard trees and beyond,
Where she took arms against her shadow,
Or harried unto the pond

The lazy geese, like a snow cloud
Dripping their snow on the green grass,
Tricking and stopping, sleepy and proud,
Who cried in goose, Alas,

For the tireless heart within the little
Lady with rod that made them rise
From their noon apple-dreams, and scuttle
Goose-fashion under the skies!

But now go the bells, and we are ready;
In one house we are sternly stopped
To say we are vexed at her brown study,
Lying so primly propped.

Blue Girls

Twirling your blue skirts, traveling the sward
Under the towers of your seminary,
Go listen to your teachers old and contrary
Without believing a word.

Tie the white fillets then about your lustrous hair
And think no more of what will come to pass
Than bluebirds that go walking on the grass
And chattering on the air.

Practice your beauty, blue girls, before it fail;
And I will cry with my loud lips and publish
Beauty which all our power shall never establish,
It is so frail.

For I could tell you a story which is true:
I know a lady with a terrible tongue,
Blear eyes fallen from blue,
All her perfections tarnished—and yet it is not long
Since she was lovelier than any of you.

Were the rich Heirs traveling incognito,
Bred too fine for the country's sweet produce
And but affecting that dog's life of pilgrims.

There used to be debate of soul and body,
The soul storming incontinent with shrew's tongue
Against what natural brilliance body had loved,
Even the green phases though deciduous
Of earth's zodiac homage to the body.

Plato, before Plotinus gentled him,
Spoke the soul's part, and though its vice is known
We're in his shadow still, and it appears
Your founders most of all the nations held
By his scandal-mongering, and established him.

Perfect was the witch foundering in water,
The blasphemer that spraddled in the stocks,
The woman branded with her sin, the whales
Of ocean taken with a psalmer's sword,
The British tea infusing the bay's water.

But they reared heads into the always clouds
And stooped to the event of war or bread,
The secular perforces and short speech
Being labors surlily done with the left hand,
The chief strength giddying with transcendent clouds.

The tangent Heavens mocked the fathers' strength,
And how the young sons know it, and study now
To take fresh conquest of the conquered earth,
But they're too strong for that, you've seem them whip
The laggard will to deeds of lunatic strength.

To incline the powerful living unto peace
With Heaven is easier now, with Earth is hard,
Yet a rare metaphysic makes them one,
A gentle Majesty, whose myrtle and rain
Enforce the fathers' gravestones unto peace.

I saw the youngling bachelors of Harvard
Lit like torches, and scrambling to disperse
Like aimless firebrands pitiful to slake,
And if there's passion enough for half their flame,
Your wisdom has done this, sages of Harvard.

Here Lies a Lady

Here lies a lady of beauty and high degree.
Of chills and fever she died, of fever and chills,
The delight of her husband, her aunt, an infant of three,
And of medicos marveling sweetly on her ills.

For either she burned, and her confident eyes would blaze,
And her fingers fly in a manner to puzzle their heads—
What was she making? Why, nothing; she sat in a maze
Of old scraps of laces, snipped into curious shreds—

Or this would pass, and the light of her fire decline
Till she lay discouraged and cold, like a stalk white and blown,
And would not open her eyes, to kisses, to wine;
The sixth of these states was her last; the cold settled down.

Sweet ladies, long may ye bloom, and toughly I hope ye may
        thole,
But was she not lucky? In flowers and lace and mourning,
In love and great honor we bade God rest her soul
After six little spaces of chill, and six of burning.

Captain Carpenter

Captain Carpenter rose up in his prime
Put on his pistols and went riding out
But had got wellnigh nowhere at that time
Till he fell in with ladies in a rout.

It was a pretty lady and all her train
That played with him so sweetly but before
An hour she'd taken a sword with all her main
And twined him of his nose for evermore.

Captain Carpenter mounted up one day
And rode straightway into a stranger rogue
That looked unchristian but be that as may
The Captain did not wait upon prologue.

But drew upon him out of his great heart
The other swung against him with a club
And cracked his two legs at the shinny part
And let him roll and stick like any tub.

Captain Carpenter rode many a time
From male and female took he sundry harms
He met the wife of Satan crying "I'm
The she-wolf bids you shall bear no more arms."

Their strokes and counters whistled in the wind
I wish he had delivered half his blows
But where she should have made off like a hind
The bitch bit off his arms at the elbows.

And Captain Carpenter parted with his ears
To a black devil that used him in this wise
O Jesus ere his threescore and ten years
Another had plucked out his sweet blue eyes.

Captain Carpenter got up on his roan
And sallied from the gate in hell's despite
I heard him asking in the grimmest tone
If any enemy yet there was to fight?

"To any adversary it is fame
If he risk to be wounded by my tongue
Or burnt in two beneath my red heart's flame
Such are the perils he is cast among.

"But if he can he has a pretty choice
From an anatomy with little to lose
Whether he cut my tongue and take my voice
Or whether it be my round red heart he choose."

It was the neatest knave that ever was seen
Stepping in perfume from his lady's bower
Who at this word put in his merry mien
And fell on Captain Carpenter like a tower.

I would not knock old fellows in the dust
But there lay Captain Carpenter on his back
His weapons were the old heart in his bust
And a blade shook between rotten teeth alack.

The rogue in scarlet and grey soon knew his mind
He wished to get his trophy and depart
With gentle apology and touch refined
He pierced him and produced the Captain's heart.

God's mercy rest on Captain Carpenter now
I thought him Sirs an honest gentleman
Citizen husband soldier and scholar enow
Let jangling kites eat of him if they can.

But God's deep curses follow after those
That shore him of his goodly nose and ears
His legs and strong arms at the two elbows
And eyes that had not watered seventy years.

The curse of hell upon the sleek upstart
That got the Captain finally on his back
And took the red red vitals of his heart
And made the kites to whet their beaks clack clack.

Piazza Piece

–I am a gentleman in a dustcoat trying
To make you hear. Your ears are soft and small
And listen to an old man not at all,
They want the young men's whispering and sighing.
But see the roses on your trellis dying
And hear the spectral singing of the moon;
For I must have my lovely lady soon,
I am a gentleman in a dustcoat trying.

–I am a lady young in beauty waiting
Until my truelove comes, and then we kiss.
But what grey man among the vines is this
Whose words are dry and faint as in a dream?
Back from my trellis, Sir, before I scream!
I am a lady young in beauty waiting.

Janet Waking

Beautifully Janet slept
Till it was deeply morning. She woke then
And thought about her dainty-feathered hen,
To see how it had kept.

One kiss she gave her mother,
Only a small one gave she to her daddy
Who would have kissed each curl of his shining baby;
No kiss at all for her brother.

"Old Chucky, old Chucky!" she cried,
Running across the world upon the grass
To Chucky's house, and listening. But alas,
Her Chucky had died.

It was a transmogrifying bee
Came droning down on Chucky's old bald head

And sat and put the poision. It scarcely bled,
But how exceedingly

And purply did the knot
Swell with the venom and communicate
Its rigor! Now the poor comb stoody up straight
But Chucky did not.

So there was Janet
Kneeling on the wet grass, crying her brown hen
(Translated far beyond the daughters of men)
To rise and walk upon it.

And weeping fast as she had breath
Janet implored us, "Wake her from her sleep!"
And would not be instructed in how deep
Was the forgetful kingdom of death.

Two in August

Two that could not have lived their single lives
As can some husbands and wives
Did something strange: they tensed their vocal cords
And attacked each other with silences and words
Like catapulted stones and arrowed knives.

Dawn was not yet; night is for loving or sleeping,
Sweet dreams or safekeeping;
Yet he of the wide brows that were used to laurel
And she, the famed for gentleness, must quarrel,
Furious both of them, and scared, and weeping.

How sleepers groan, twitch, wake to such a mood
Is not well understood,
Nor why two entities grown almost one
Should rend and murder trying to get undone,
With individual tigers in their blood.

She in terror fled from the marriage chamber
Circuiting the dark rooms like a string of amber
Round and round and back,
And would not light one lamp against the black,
And heard the clock that changed: Remember, Remember.

And he must tread barefooted the dim lawn,
Soon he was up and gone;
High in the trees the night-mastered birds were crying
With fear upon their tongues, no singing nor flying
Which are their lovely attitudes by dawn.

Whether those bird-cries were of heaven or hell
There is no way to tell;
In the long ditch of darkness the man walked
Under the hackberry trees where the birds talked
With words too sad and strange to syllable.

Antique Harvesters

(Scene: Of the Mississippi the bank sinister, and of
the Ohio the bank sinister.)

Tawny are the leaves turned but they still hold,
And it is harvest; what shall this land produce?
A meager hill of kernels, a runnel of juice;
Declension looks from our land, it is old.
Therefore let us assemble, dry, grey, spare,
And mild as yellow air.

"I hear the croak of a raven's funeral wing."
The young men would be joying in the song
Of passionate birds; their memories are not long.
What is it thus rehearsed in sable? "Nothing."
Trust not but the old endure, and shall be older
Than the scornful beholder.

We pluck the spindling ears and gather the corn.
One spot has special yield? "On this spot stood
Heroes and drenched it with their only blood."
And talk meets talk, as echoes from the horn
Of the hunter—echoes are the old men's arts,
Ample are the chambers of their hearts.

Here come the hunters, keepers of a rite;
The horn, the hounds, the lank mares coursing by
Straddled with archetypes of chivalry;
And the fox, lovely ritualist, in flight
Offering his unearthly ghost to quarry;
And the fields, themselves to harry.

Resume, harvesters. The treasure is full bronze
Which you will garner for the Lady, and the moon
Could tinge it no yellower than does this noon;
But grey will quench it shortly—the field, men, stones.
Pluck fast, dreamers; prove as you amble slowly
Not less than men, not wholly.

Bare the arm, dainty youths, bend the knees
Under bronze burdens. And by an autumn tone
As by a grey, as by a green, you will have known
Your famous Lady's image; for so have these;
And if one say that easily will your hands
More prosper in other lands,

Angry as wasp-music be your cry then:
"Forsake the Proud Lady, of the heart of fire,
The look of snow, to the praise of a dwindled choir,
Song of degenerate specters that were men?
The sons of the fathers shall keep her, worthy of
What these have done in love."

True, it is said of our Lady, she ageth.
But see, if you peep shrewdly, she hath not stooped;
Take no thought of her servitors that have drooped,

For we are nothing; and if one talk of death—
Why, the ribs of the earth subsist frail as a breath
If but God wearieth.

Dog

Cock-a-doodle-doo the brass-lined rooster says,
Brekekekex intones the fat Greek frog—
These fantasies do not terrify me as
The bow-wow-wow of dog.

I had a little doggie who used to sit and beg,
A pretty little creature with tears in his eyes
And anomalous hand extended on his leg;
Housebroken was my Huendchen, and so wise.

Booms the voice of a big dog like a bell.
But Fido sits at dusk on Madam's lap
And, bored beyond his tongue's poor skill to tell,
Rehearses his pink paradigm, To yap.

However. Up the lane the tender bull
Proceeds unto his kine; he yearns for them,
Whose eyes adore him and are beautiful;
Love speeds him and no treason nor mayhem.

But, on arriving at the gap in the fence,
Behold! again the ubiquitous hairy dog,
Like a numerous army rattling the battlements
With shout, though it is but his monologue,
With a lion's courage and a bee's virulence
Though he is but one dog.

Shrill is the fury of the proud red bull,
His knees quiver, and the honeysuckle vine
Expires with anguish as his voice, terrible,
Cries, "What do you want of my twenty lady kine?"

Ah, nothing doubtless; yet his dog's fang is keen,
His dog's heart cannot suffer these marriage rites
Enacted in the dark if they are obscene;
Misogynist, censorious of delights.

Now the air trembles to the sorrowing Moo
Of twenty blameless ladies of the mead
Fearing their lord's precarious set-to.
It is the sunset and the heavens bleed.

The hooves of the red bull slither the claybank
And cut the green tendrils of the vine; his horn
Slices the young birch unto splinter and shank
But lunging leaves the bitch's boy untorn.

Across the red sky comes master, Hodge by name,
Upright, biped, tall-browed, and self-assured,
In his hand a cudgel, in his cold eye a flame:
"Have I beat my dog so sore and he is not cured?"

His stick and stone and curse rain on the brute
That pipped his bull of gentle pedigree
Till the leonine smarts with pain and disrepute
And the bovine weeps in the bosom of his family.

Old Hodge stays not his hand, but whips to kennel
The renegade. God's peace betide the souls
Of the pure in heart. But in the box that fennel
Grows round are two red eyes that stare like coals.

The Equilibrists

Full of her long white arms and milky skin
He had a thousand times remembered sin.
Alone in the press of people traveled he,
Minding her jacinth, and myrrh, and ivory.

Mouth he remembered: the quaint orifice
From which came heat that flamed upon the kiss,
Till cold words came down spiral from the head,
Grey doves from the officious tower illsped.

Body: it was a white field ready for love,
On her body's field, with the gaunt tower above,
The lilies grew, beseeching him to take,
If he would pluck and wear them, bruise and break.

Eyes talking: Never mind the cruel words,
Embrace my flowers, but not embrace the swords.
But what they said, the doves came straightway flying
And unsaid: Honor, Honor, they came crying.

Importunate her doves. Too pure, too wise,
Clambering on his shoulder, saying, Arise,
Leave me now, and never let us meet,
Eternal distance now command thy feet.

Predicament indeed, which thus discovers
Honor among thieves, Honor between lovers.
O such a little word is Honor, they feel!
But the grey word is between them cold as steel.

At length I saw these lovers fully were come
Into their torture of equilibrium;
Dreadfully had forsworn each other, and yet
They were bound each to each, and they did not forget.

And rigid as two painful stars, and twirled
About the clustered night their prison world,
They burned with fierce love always to come near,
But Honor beat them back and kept them clear.

Ah, the strict lovers, they are ruined now!
I cried in anger. But with puddled brow
Devising for those gibbeted and brave
Came I descanting: Man, what would you have?

For spin your period out, and draw your breath,
A kinder saeculum begins with Death.
Would you ascend to Heaven and bodiless dwell?
Or take your bodies honorless to Hell?

In Heaven you have heard no marriage is,
No white flesh tinder to your lecheries,
Your male and female tissue sweetly shaped
Sublimed away, and furious blood escaped.

Great lovers lie in Hell, the stubborn ones
Infatuate of the flesh upon the bones;
Stuprate, they rend each other when they kiss,
The pieces kiss again, no end to this.

But still I watched them spinning, orbited nice.
Their flames were not more radiant than their ice.
I dug in the quiet earth and wrought the tomb
And made these lines to memorize their doom:–

Epitaph

Equilibrists lie here; stranger, tread light;
Close, but untouching in each other's sight;
Mouldered the lips and ashy the tall skull,
Let them lie perilous and beautiful.

Painted Head

By dark severance the apparition head
Smiles from the air a capital on no
Column or a Platonic perhaps head
On a canvas sky depending from nothing;

Stirs up an old illusion of grandeur
By tickling the instinct of heads to be

Absolute and to try decapitation
And to play truant from the body bush;

But too happy and beautiful for those sorts
Of head (homekeeping heads are happiest)
Discovers maybe thirty unwidowed years
Of not dishonoring the faithful stem;

Is nameless and has authored for the evil
Historian headhunters neither book
Nor state and is therefore distinct from tart
Heads with crowns and guilty gallery heads;

So that the extravagant device of art
Unhousing by abstraction this once head
Was capital irony by a loving hand
That knew the no treason of a head like this;

Makes repentance in an unlovely head
For having vinegarly traduced the flesh
Till, the hurt flesh recusing, the hard egg
Is shrunken to its own deathlike surface;

And an image thus. The body bears the head
(So hardly one they terribly are two)
Feeds and obeys and unto please what end?
Not to the glory of tyrant head but to

The increase of body. Beauty is of body.
The flesh contouring shallowly on a head
Is a rock-garden needing body's love
And best bodiness to colorify

The big blue birds sitting and sea-shell flats
And caves, and on the iron acropolis
To spread the hyacinthine hair and rear
The olive garden for the nightingales.

JOHN PEALE BISHOP   [1892-1941]

John Peale Bishop was born in Charles Town, West Virginia. He attended the Mercersburg Academy in Pennsylvania and graduated from Princeton University in 1917. While there he became friends with F. Scott Fitzgerald and Edmund Wilson. He served in the first World War as a Lieutenant in the infantry. When he returned to the United States, he joined the staff of *Vanity Fair* and eventually succeeded Edmund Wilson as the publication's managing editor. In subsequent years, he worked for Paramount Pictures and lived off and on in France. In 1933, he settled in Cape Cod where he devoted most of his attention to critical writing; eight years later, he moved to New York where he took a government job overseeing the publication of South American anthologies. Four years after his death, Allen Tate put together an edition of his *Collected Poems*.

Always, from My First Boyhood

Always, from my first boyhood,
I have known how, lying awake in a straightened
Nakedness–curtains of rain drawn at the window–
To summon from dimness beautiful bodies,
While, over my iron pallet, the painful
Windiness of lilacs spread an
Impalpable coverlet.

Bodies of young men centaured on horses:
Pliant and tawny as leopards, they ride
Over a ground made spongy by April and rains,
Against the drawn lines of a forest
Misty as rain, clouded with torn green;
Their thighs are pressed like bronze to the gleaming
White flanks of the horses; stirrupless, their feet
Toe in abandon; for their eyes are upraised
Where, blue and afar, the jutted mountains
Renew their ancient march in sunrise.

Scarcely has the brittle bickering of twigs
Subsided from their hoofbeats, when I have, with words,
Disenchanted from the grey web of the wood's edge
The tenuous, rose-frosted beauty of women.
Their mouths are claret-wet from some mystery,
Virginal, awful, performed in the forest;
Or else they have seen, by the yellow flame of crocuses,

The flushed and long-sought touching of lovers.
For now, with burnt savage hair outshaken,
Tremulous, exulted, they front the east wind,
Complaining toward the curveting fading horsemen.

Always it is the same: the fixed, blue-radiant
Mountains; the horsemen on horses, the young men
Staring afar off, and the women crying, crying–
The retreating lure and the sinuous beautiful bodies.

So, beginning at midnight, I am as one
Steeped in intolerable wine, and lie
Throbbing; exhausted only when the arid dawn
Cracks its light on the fissile planes of the mirror.

In the Dordogne

We stood up before day
and shaved by metal mirrors
in the faint flame of a faulty candle.

And we hurried down the wide stone stairs
with a clirr of spur chains
on stone. And we thought
when the cocks crew
that the ghosts of a dead dawn
would rise and be off. But they stayed
under the window, crouched on the staircase,
the window now the color of morning.

The colonel asleep in the bed of Sully
slept on: but we descended
and saw in a niche in the white wall
a Virgin and child, serene
who were stones: we saw sycamores:
three aged mages
scattering gifts of gold.
But when the wind blew, there were autumn odors
and the shadowed trees
had the dapplings of young fawns.

And each day one died or another
died: each week we sent out thousands
that returned by hundreds
wounded or gassed. And those that died
we buried close to the old wall
within a stone's throw of Perigord
under the tower of the troubadours.

And because we had courage;
because there was courage and youth
ready to be wasted; because we endured
and were prepared for all endurance;
we thought something must come of it:
that the Virgin would raise her child and smile;
the trees gather up their gold and go;
that courage would avail something
and something we had never lost
be regained through wastage, by dying,
by burying the others under the English tower.

The colonel slept on in the bed of Sully
under the ravelling curtains: the leaves fell
and were blown away: the young men rotted
under the shadow of the tower
in a land of small clear silent streams
where the coming on of evening is
the letting down of blue and azure veils
over the clear and silent streams
delicately bordered by poplars.

ARCHIBALD MACLEISH   [1892–1982]

Archibald MacLeish was born in Glencoe, Illinois. He attended Yale University where he excelled in sports and was chairman of the *Yale Literary Monthly*. He served in World War I and rose to the rank of captain in the artillery. Later he went to Harvard Law School and graduated at the head of his class. Yet after only a few years of practicing law in Boston, he gave it up and moved to Paris with his wife and children in order to devote all his time to writing poetry. During this period, he produced such volumes as *The Happy Marriage* (1924), *The Pot of Earth* (1925), *Streets on the Moon* (1926), and *The Hamlet of A. MacLeish* (1928). He returned to the U.S. to research the Spanish conquest of Mexico, and the result, *Conquistador* (1932), won him a Pulitzer prize. From 1920–39, he was a member of the editorial board of *Fortune* magazine; from 1939-44, he served as Librarian of Congress. He was one of the most influential advisers during the Roosevelt administration, serving variously as Assistant Director of the Office of Facts and Figures, Assistant Director of War Information, and Assistant Secretary of State. He helped draft the UNESCO Constitution.

Many of MacLeish's poems deal in a direct and powerful way with the political and social situations of his time. Although he was strongly influenced by Ezra Pound and T.S. Eliot, he eventually came to oppose the scholastic poetry they espoused because it was too far removed from the pressing concerns of society. MacLeish asserted that the great poets of the past—Chaucer, Shakespeare, Milton—did not retreat from social and political issues, and it was the duty of modern poets to similarly involve themselves with their society. MacLeish's *Collected Poems* (1952) won a Pulitzer prize and his poetic drama, *J.B.*, based on the Book of Job, was a Broadway success in 1957.

Memorial Rain

For Kenneth MacLeish, 1894-1918

Ambassador Puser the ambassador
Reminds himself in French, felicitous tongue,
What these (young men no longer) lie here for
In rows that once, and somewhere else, were young. . .

All night in Brussels the wind had tugged at my door:
I had heard the wind at my door and the trees strung
Taut, and to me who had never been before
In that country it was a strange wind, blowing

Steadily, stiffening the walls, the floor,
The roof of my room. I had not slept for knowing
He too, dead, was a stranger in that land
And felt beneath the earth in the wind's flowing
A tightening of roots and would not understand,
Remembering lake winds in Illinois,
That strange wind. I had felt his bones in the sand
Listening.

                    . . . *Reflects that these enjoy*
Their country's gratitude, that deep repose,
That peace no pain can break, no hurt destroy,
That rest, that sleep . . .

                    At Ghent the wind rose.
There was a smell of rain and a heavy drag
Of wind in the hedges but not as the wind blows
Over fresh water when the waves lag
Foaming and the willows huddle and it will rain:
I felt him waiting.

          . . . *Indicates the flag*
Which (may he say) enisles in Flanders plain
This little field these happy, happy dead
Have made America . . .

In the ripe grain
The wind coiled glistening, darted, fled,
Dragging its heavy body: at Waereghem
The wind coiled in the grass above his head:
Waiting–listening . . .

> . . . *Dedicates to them*
> *This earth their bones have hallowed, this last gift*
> *A Grateful country* . . .

Under the dry grass stem
The words are blurred, are thickened, the words sift
Confused by the rasp of the wind, by the thin grating
Of ants under the grass, the minute shift
And tumble of dusty sand separating
From dusty sand. The roots of the grass strain,
Tighten, the earth is rigid, waits–he is waiting–

And suddenly, and all at once, the rain!

The living scatter, they run into houses, the wind
Is trampled under the rain, shakes free, is again
Trampled. The rain gathers, running in thinned

Spurts of water that ravel in the dry sand,
Seeping in the sand under the grass roots, seeping
Between cracked boards to the bones of a clenched hand:
The earth relaxes, loosens; he is sleeping,
He rests, he is quiet, he sleeps in a strange land.

Ars Poetica

A poem should be palpable and mute
As a globed fruit

Dumb
As old medallions to the thumb

Silent as the sleeve-worn stone
Of casement ledges where the moss has grown—

A poem should be wordless
As the flight of birds
                    *   *   *

A poem should be motionless in time
As the moon climbs

Leaving, as the moon releases
Twig by twig the night-entangled trees,

Leaving, as the moon behind the winter leaves,
Memory by memory the mind—

A poem should be motionless in time
As the moon climbs
                    *   *   *

A poem should be equal to:
Not true

For all the history of grief
An empty doorway and a maple leaf

For love
The leaning grasses and two lights above the sea—

A poem should not mean
But be

You, Andrew Marvell

And here face down beneath the sun
And here upon earth's noonward height
To feel the always coming on
The always rising of the night:

To feel creep up the curving east
The earthly chill of dusk and slow
Upon those under lands the vast
And ever climbing shadow grow

And strange at Ecbatan the trees
Take leaf by leaf the evening strange
The flooding dark about their knees
The mountains over Persia change

And now at Kermanshah the gate
Dark empty and the withered grass
And through the twilight now the late
Few travelers in the westward pass

And Baghdad darken and the bridge
Across the silent river gone
And through Arabia the edge
Of evening widen and steal on

And deepen on Palmyra's street
The wheel rut in the ruined stone
And Lebanon fade out and Crete
High through the clouds and overblown

And over Sicily the air
Still flashing with the landward gulls
And loom and slowly disappear
The sails above the shadowy hulls

And Spain go under and the shore
Of Africa the gilded sand

And evening vanish and no more
The low pale light across that land

Nor now the long light on the sea:

And here face downward in the sun
To feel how swift how secretly
The shadow of the night comes on . . .

The End of the World

Quite unexpectedly as Vasserot
The armless ambidextrian was lighting
A match between his great and second toe
And Ralph the lion was engaged in biting
The neck of Madame Sossman while the drum
Pointed, and Teeny was about to cough
In waltz-time swinging Jocko by the thumb—
Quite unexpectedly the top blew off:
And there, there overhead, there, there, hung over
Those thousands of white faces, those dazed eyes,
There in the starless dark, the poise, the hover,
There with vast wings across the canceled skies,
There in the sudden blackness, the black pall
Of nothing, nothing, nothing—nothing at all.

Epistle to Be Left in the Earth

. . . It is colder now
            there are many stars
                        we are drifting
North by the Great Bear
                        the leaves are falling
The water is stone in the scooped rocks
                        to southward

Red sun gray air
       the crows are
Slow on their crooked wings
               the jays have left us
Long since we passed the flares of Orion
Each man believes in his heart he will die
Many have written last thoughts and last letters
None know if our deaths are now or forever
None know if this wandering earth will be found

We lie down and the snow covers our garments
I pray you
       you (if any open this writing)
Make in your mouths the words that were our names
I will tell you all we have learned
             I will tell you everything
The earth is round
       there are springs under the orchards
The loam cuts with a blunt knife
          beware of
Elms in thunder
       the lights in the sky are stars
We think they do not see
         we think also
The trees do not know nor the leaves of the grasses
                hear us

The birds too are ignorant
          Do not listen
Do not stand at dark in the open windows
We before you have heard this
        they are voices
They are not words at all but the wind rising
Also none among us has seen God
(. . . We have thought often
The flaws of sun in the late and driving weather
Pointed to one tree but it was not so)
As for the nights I warn you the nights are dangerous
The wind changes at night and the dreams come

It is very cold
        there are strange stars near Arcturus

Voices are crying an unknown name in the sky

The Reconciliation

Time like the repetitions of a child's piano
Brings me the room again the shallow lamp the love
The night the silence the slow bell the echoed answer.

By no thing here or lacking can the eyes discover
The hundred winter evenings that have gone between
Nor know for sure the night is this and not that other.

The room is here the lamp is here: the mirror's leaning
Searches the same deep shadow where her knees were caught:
All these are here within the room as I have seen them.

Time has restored them all as in that rainy autumn:
Even the echoes of that night return to this–
All as they were when first the earthy evening brought them.

Between this night and that there is no human distance:
There is no space an arm could not out-reach by much–
And yet the stars most far apart are not more distant.

Between my hand that touched and her soft breast that touches
The irremediable past as deep as tone:
Wider than water: like all land and ocean stretches:

We touch and by that touching farness are alone.

Speech to a Crowd

Tell me, my patient friends–awaiters of messages–
From what other shore: from what stranger:
Whence was the word to come? Who was to lesson you?

Listeners under a child's crib in a manger–
Listeners once by the oracles: now by the transoms–
Whom are you waiting for? Who do you think will explain?

Listeners thousands of years and still no answer–
Writers at night to Miss Lonely-Hearts: awkward spellers–
Open your eyes! There is only earth and the man!

There is only you: there is no one else on the telephone:
No one else is on the air to whisper:
No one else but you will push the bell.

No one knows if you don't: neither ships
Nor landing-fields decode the dark between:
You have your eyes and what your eyes see *is*.

The earth you see is really the earth you are seeing:
The sun is truly excellent: truly warm:
Women are beautiful as you have seen them–

Their breasts (believe it) like cooing of doves in a portico:
They bear at their breasts tenderness softly. Look at them!
Look at yourselves. You are strong. You are well formed.

Look at the world–the world you never took!
It is really true you may live in the world heedlessly:
Why do you wait to read it in a book then?

Write it yourselves! Write to yourselves if you need to!
Tell yourselves there is sun and the sun will rise:
Tell yourselves the earth has food to feed you:–

Let the dead men say that men must die!
Who better than you can know what death is?
How can a bone or a broken body surmise it?

Let the dead shriek with their whispering breath:
Laugh at them! Say the murdered gods may wake
But we who work have end of work together:

Tell yourselves the earth is yours to take!

Waiting for messages out of the dark you were poor.
The world was always yours: you will not take it.

Immortal Autumn

I speak this poem now with grave and level voice
In praise of autumn, of the far-horn-winding fall.

I praise the flower-barren fields, the clouds, the tall
Unanswering branches where the wind makes sullen noise.

I praise the fall: it is the human season.
                                        Now
No more the foreign sun does meddle at our earth,
Enforce the green and bring the fallow land to birth,
Nor winter yet weigh all with silence the pine bough,

But now in autumn with the black and outcast crows
Share we the spacious world: the whispering year is gone:
There is more room to live now: the once secret dawn
Comes late by daylight and the dark unguarded goes.

Between the mutinous brave burning of the leaves
And winter's covering of our hearts with his deep snow
We are alone: there are no evening birds: we know
The naked moon: the tame stars circle at our eaves.

It is the human season. On this sterile air
Do words outcarry breath: the sound goes on and on.
I hear a dead man's cry from autumn long since gone.

I cry to you beyond upon this bitter air.

Tourist Death

For Sylvia Beach

I promise you these days and an understanding
Of light in the twigs after sunfall.
                              Do you ask to descend
At dawn in a new world with wet on the pavements
And a yawning cat and the fresh odor of dew
And red geraniums under the station windows
And doors wide and brooms and sheets on the railing
And a whistling boy and the sun like shellac on the street?

Do you ask to embark at night at the third hour
Sliding away in the dark and the sails of the fishermen
Slack in the light of the lanterns and black seas
And the tide going down and the splash and drip of the hawser?

Do you ask something to happen as spring does
In a night in a small time and nothing the same again?
Life is neither a prize box nor a terminus.
Life is a haft that has fitted the palms of many,
Dark as the helved oak,
                              with sweat bitter,
Browned by numerous hands:
                              Death is the rest of it.
Death is the same bones and the trees nearer.
Death is a serious thing like the loam smell
Of the plowed earth in the fall.
                              Death is here:
Not in another place, not among strangers.

Death is under the moon here and the rain.
I promise you old signs and a recognition
Of sun in the seething grass and the wind's rising.

Do you ask more?
                    Do you ask to travel for ever?

Invocation to the Social Muse

Señora, it is true the Greeks are dead.

It is true also that we here are Americans:
That we use the machines: that a sight of the god is unusual
That more people have more thoughts: that there are

Progress and science and tractors and revolutions and
Marx and the wars more antiseptic and murderous
And music in every home: there is also Hoover.

Does the lady suggest we should write it out in The Word?
Does Madame recall our responsibilities? We are
Whores, Fräulein: poets, Fräulein, are persons of

Known vocation following troops: they must sleep with
Stragglers from either prince and of both views.
The rules permit them to further the business of neither.

It is also strictly forbidden to mix in maneuvers.
Those that infringe are inflated with praise on the plazas—
Their bones are resultantly afterwards found under newspapers.

Preferring life with the sons to death with the fathers,
We also doubt on the record whether the sons
Will still be shouting around with the same huzzas—

For we hope Lady to live to lie with the youngest.
There are only a handful of things a man likes,
Generation to generation, hungry or

Well fed: the earth's one: life's
One: Mister Morgan is not one.

There is nothing worse for our trade than to be in style.

He that goes naked goes further at last than another.
Wrap the bard in a flag or a school and they'll jimmy his
Door down and be thick in his bed—for a month:

(Who recalls the address now of the Imagists?)
But the naked man has always his own nakedness.
People remember forever his live limbs.

They may drive him out of the camps but one will take him.
They may stop his tongue on his teeth with a rope's argu-
        ment—
He will lie in a house and be warm when they are shaking.

Besides, Tovarishch, how to embrace an army?
How to take to one's chamber a million souls?
How to conceive in the name of a column of marchers?

The things of the poet are done to a man alone
As the things of love are done—or of death when he hears the
Step withdraw on the stair and the clock tick only.

Neither his class nor his kind nor his trade may come near him
There where he lies on his left arm and will die,
Nor his class nor his kind nor his trade when the blood is
        jeering

And his knee's in the soft of the bed where his love lies.

I remind you, Barinya, the life of the poet is hard—
A hardy life with a boot as quick as a fiver:

Is it just to demand of us also to bear arms?

GENEVIEVE TAGGARD [1894-1948]

Born in Waitsburg, Washington, Genevieve Taggard spent nearly all of her childhood and adolescence in Hawaii. She graduated from the University of California in 1919, where she had edited the school's literary magazine. In 1921, she and a group of other poets founded *The Measure*, a journal of verse. Her first two volumes of poetry appeared soon thereafter: *For Eager Lovers* (1922) and *Hawaiian Hilltop* (1923). In 1930, she published *The Life and Mind of Emily Dickinson,* a critical biography, and, in 1931, she joined the faculty of Bennington College. In later years, she wrote lyrics for such composers as Aaron Copland and Roy Harris. Her verse is noted for its traditional and metaphysical nature.

With Child

Now I am slow and placid, fond of sun,
Like a sleek beast, or a worn one:
No slim and languid girl—not glad
With the windy trip I once had,
But velvet-footed, musing of my own,
Torpid, mellow, stupid as a stone.

You cleft me with your beauty's pulse, and
    now
Your pulse has taken body. Care not how
The old grace goes, how heavy I am grown,
Big with this loneliness, how you alone
Ponder our love. Touch my feet and feel
How earth tingles, teeming at my heel!
Earth's urge, not mine—my little death, not
    hers;
And the pure beauty yearns and stirs.
It does not heed our ecstasies, it turns
With secrets of its own, its own concerns,
Toward a windy world of its own, toward
    stark
And solitary places. In the dark,
Defiant even now, it tugs and moans
To be untangled from these mother's bones.

Solar Myth

(Maui, the dutiful son and great hero, yields to his mother's
entreaty and adjusts the center of the universe to her conven-
ience. The days are too short for drying tapa. He is persuaded to
slow down the speed of the spider-sun with a lasso of sisal rope.)

The golden spider of the sky
Leaped from the crater's rim;
And all the winds of morning rose
And spread, and followed him.

The circle of the day swept out,
His vast and splendid path;
The purple sea spumed in the west
His humid evening bath.

Thrice twenty mighty legs he had,
And over earth there passed
Shadows daily whipping by,
Faster, faster, fast . . .

For daily did he wax more swift,
And daily did he run
The span of heaven to the sea,
A lusty, rebel sun.

Then Maui's mother came to him
With weight of household woes:
"I cannot get my tapa dry
Before the daylight goes.

"Mornings I rise and spread with care
My tapa on the grass;
Evenings I gather it again
A damp and sodden mass."

Then Maui rose and climbed at night
The mountain. Dim and deep
Within the crater's bowl he saw
The sprawling sun asleep.

He looped his ropes, the mighty man,
He whirled his sisal cords;
They whistled like a hurricane
And cut the air like swords.

Up sprang the spider. Maui hurled
His lasso after him.
The spider fled. Great Maui stood
Firm on the mountain-rim.

The spider dipped and swerved and pulled
But struggle as he might,
Around one-half his whirl of leg
The sisal ropes cut tight.

He broke them off, the mighty man,
He dropped them in the sea,
Where there had once been sixty legs
There now were thirty-three.

Maui counted them, and took
The pathway home; and came
Back to his mother, brooding,–strode
Like a lost man, and lame.

The tarnished spider of the sky
Limped slowly over heaven,
And with his going mourned and moaned
The missing twenty-seven.

On with a hollow voice he moaned,
Poured out his hollow woe;
Over each day the sound of him
Bellowing, went below.

Maui saw the gulls swarm up
And scream and settle on
The carcass of the limping thing
That once had been the sun.

But still he thought at length to have
His mother satisfied.
"Can't you put back his legs again
Now all my tapa's dried?"

"The days are long and dull," she said,
"I love to see them skim." . . .
Wearily the old sun shook
The black birds off of him.

American Farm, 1934

Space is too full. Did nothing happen here?
Skin of poor life cast off. These pods and shards
Rattle in the old house, rock with the old rocker,
Tick with the old clock, clutter the mantel.
Waste of disregarded trifles crooked as old crochet
On tabourets of wicker. Mute boredom of hoarding
Poor objects. These outlive water sluicing in cracks to
    join
The destroying river, the large Mississippi; or the tornado
Twisting dishes and beds and bird-cages into droppings
    of cloud.
The hard odd thing surviving precariously, once of some
    value
Brought home bright from the store in manila paper,
Now under the foot of the cow, caught in a crevice.
One old shoe, feminine, rotted with damp, one worn tire,
Crop of tin cans, torn harness, nails, links of a chain,–
Edge of a dress, wrappings of contraceptives, trinkets,
Fans spread, sick pink, and a skillet full of mould,
Bottles in cobwebs, butter-nuts–and the copperheads,
Night-feeders, who run their evil bellies in and out
Weaving a fabric of limbo for the devil of limbo;
Droppings of swallows, baked mud of wasps, confetti
Of the mouse nest, ancient cow-dung frozen,
Jumble of items, lost from use, with rusty tools,
Calendars, apple-cores, white sick grasses, gear from the
    stables,
Skull of a cow in the mud, with the stem of dead cabbage.
Part of the spine and the ribs, in the rot of swill mud. This
Array of limbo, once a part of swart labor, rusted now,
In every house, in every attic piled. Oh palsied people!
Under the weeds of the outhouse something one never
Picks up or burns; flung away. Let it lie; let it bleach.
Ironic and sinister junk filling a corner. If men vacate,
Prized or unprized, it jests with neglect.
Under the porch the kitten goes and returns,

Masked with small dirt. Odd objects in sheds and shelves,
And the stale air of bed-rooms, stink of stained bureaus.
Flies buzzing in bottles; vocal tone of no meaning.
No wonder our farms are dark and our dreams take these
    shapes.
Thistles mock all, growing out of rubbish
In a heap of broken glass with last year's soot.
Implacable divine rubbish prevails. Possessors of things
Look at the junk heap for an hour. Gnarled idle hands
Find ticks in the pelt of the dog, turn over a plank.
This parasite clutter invades sense and seems to breed
A like in our minds. Wind, water, sun;–it survives.
The whole sad place scales to the thistle and petty litter.
Neglect laughs in the fallen barns and the shutters broken
Hanging on a wailing hinge. Generations of wind
Owe you obeisance. You win. No man will war with you.
He has you in him; his hand trembles; he rights
The front acre while the wife tidies the parlour.
Economy, economy! Who'll till this land?

The Little Girl with Bands on Her Teeth

I was far forward on the plain, the burning swamp,
When the child called. And she was far behind.
She was not my child, my charge. By chance I heard.
She called from the first delusive fork. She cried her dis-
    tress.
For me, much walking lay ahead, my stint, much walking.
The very gist of the problem. And nightfall. And I in a
    swamp.
I heard, could not go on; she cried; she called me back.

Then my temper was short, for remember I split my duty
    in two.
And cry is the concern of all; we are all in a swamp . . .
    this was discovered.
But the old fables of ruin decline. . . . I deserted myself.

Once to go back is nothing; one return matters not,
But daily to traverse the great gap of our ages,
Daily to go on, and daily return the triple mile!
And she less able to go . . . to see her less able.

Good Christopher, the saint! Bless the past for such pity.
The windows of pity shine, holy and vapid.
We need an essential plinth in the gap of that pity.
Farewell, Child. Try to hear my bleak meaning.
We will build a fine house, if we finish this journey.
My specious pride dies. If you wish, call me evil.
I travel the risk of the end. O perilous love.

Try Tropic

On the Properties of Nature for Healing an
Illness

Try tropic for your balm,
Try storm,
And after storm, calm.
Try snow of heaven, heavy, soft, and slow,
Brilliant and warm.
Nothing will help, and nothing do much
   harm.

Drink iron from rare springs; follow the sun;
Go far
To get the beam of some medicinal star;
Or in your anguish run
The gauntlet of all zones to an ultimate one.
Fever and chill
Punish you still,
Earth has no zone to work against your ill.

Burn in the jeweled desert with the toad.
Catch lace

In evening mist across your haunted face;
Or walk in upper air the slanted road.
It will not lift that load;
Nor will large seas undo your subtle ill.

Nothing can cure and nothing kill
What ails your eyes, what cuts your pulse in
    two,
And not kill you.

Dilemma of the Elm

In summer elms are made for me.
I walk ignoring them and they
Ignore my walking in a way
I like in any elegant tree.

Fountain of the elm is shape
For something I have felt and said. . . .
In winter to hear the lonely scrape
Of rooty branches overhead

Should make me only half believe
An elm had ever a frond of green–
Faced by the absence of a leaf
Forget the fair elms I have seen.

(A wiry fountain, black upon
The little landscape, pale-blue with snow–
Elm of my summer, obscurely gone
To leave me another elm to know.)

Instead, I paint it with my thought,
Not knowing, hardly, that I do;
The elm comes back I had forgot
I see it green, absurdly new,

Grotesquely growing in the snow.
In winter an elm's a double tree;
In winter all elms trouble me.

But in summer elms are made for me.
I can ignore the way they grow.

E. E. CUMMINGS [1894-1962]

Edward Estlin Cummings was born into a cultured family in Cambridge, Massachusetts. His father, a Congregational minister, taught English literature and social ethics at Harvard University. Cummings himself attended Harvard, where he received his M.A. in 1916. Even before the United States entered the first World War, Cummings went to France where he served as a driver in the Norton Harjes Ambulance Corps. Due to the mistake of a military official, Cummings and a friend were confined for three months in a military detention camp. He chronicled this experience in *The Enormous Room*, which was published in 1922, and immediately made him famous. From 1921-23 Cummings lived in Paris and returned there many times throughout his life. He published his first book of poems, *Tulips and Chimneys* in 1923 and settled in a Greenwich Village studio the following year. This was to remain his primary residence for the rest of his life.

Cummings was a painter as well as a poet, he would paint by day and write in the evenings. (He exhibited his work as early as 1919; his first major show was in Cleveland in 1931.) His poetry is by turns witty, playful, poignant, and satiric. Time and again, he renounces moral hypocrisy, conformity, prejudice, and warfare, but he is probably best known for his formal experiments, which were often radically innovative. Although many of his poems are reworkings of the traditional sonnet form, his verse is typified by wildly imaginative assaults on conventional syntax, punctuation, and typography. It was a favorite device of his to use nouns as verbs. By midcentury, Cummings was one of the most popular poets among high school and college students; in 1950, the Academy of American Poets gave him an award for "great achievement".

anyone lived in a pretty how town

anyone lived in a pretty how town
(with up so floating many bells down)
spring summer autumn winter
he sang his didn't he danced his did.

Women and men (both little and small)
cared for anyone not at all
they sowed their isn't they reaped their same
sun moon stars rain

children guessed (but only a few
and down they forgot as up they grew
autumn winter spring summer)
that noone loved him more by more

when by now and tree by leaf
she laughed his joy she cried his grief
bird by snow and stir by still
anyone's any was all to her

someones married their everyones
laughed their cryings and did their dance
(sleep wake hope and then) they
said their nevers they slept their dream

stars rain sun moon
(and only the snow can begin to explain
how children are apt to forget to remember
with up so floating many bells down)

one day anyone died i guess
(and noone stooped to kiss his face)
busy folk buried them side by side
little by little and was by was

all by all and deep by deep
and more by more they dream their sleep
noone and anyone earth by april
wish by spirit and if by yes.

Women and men (both dong and ding)
summer autumn winter spring
reaped their sowing and went their came
sun moon stars rain

my father moved through dooms of love

my father moved through dooms of love
through sames of am through haves of give,
singing each morning out of each night
my father moved through depths of height

this motionless forgetful where
turned at his glance to shining here;
that if(so timid air is firm)
under his eyes would stir and squirm

newly as from unburied which
floats the first who,his april touch
drove sleeping selves to swarm their fates
woke dreamers to their ghostly roots

and should some why completely weep
my father's fingers brought her sleep:
vainly no smallest voice might cry
for he could feel the mountains grow.

Lifting the valleys of the sea
my father moved through griefs of joy;
praised a forehead called the moon
singing desire into begin

joy was his song and joy so pure
a heart of star by him could steer
and pure so now and now so yes
the wrists of twilight would rejoice

keen as midsummer's keen beyond
conceiving mind of sun will stand,
so strictly(over utmost him
so hugely)stood my father's dream

his flesh was flesh his blood was blood:
no hungry man but wished him food;
no cripple wouldn't creep one mile
uphill to only see him smile.

Scorning the pomp of must and shall
my father moved through dooms of feel;
his anger was as right as rain
his pity was as green as grain

septembering arms of year extend
less humbly wealth to foe and friend
than he to foolish and to wise
offered immeasurable is

proudly and(by octobering flame
beckoned)as earth will downward climb,
so naked for immortal work
his shoulders marched against the dark

his sorrow was as true as bread:
no liar looked him in the head;
if every friend became his foe
he'd laugh and build a world with snow.

My father moved through theys of we,
singing each new leaf out of each tree
(and every child was sure that spring
danced when she heard my father sing)

then let men kill which cannot share,
let blood and flesh be mud and mire,
scheming imagine,passion willed,
freedom a drug that's bought and sold

giving to steal and cruel kind,
a heart to fear, to doubt a mind,
to differ a disease of same,
conform the pinnacle of am

though dull were all we taste as bright,
bitter all utterly things sweet,
maggoty minus and dumb death
all we inherit,all bequeath

and nothing quite so least as truth
–i say though hate were why men breathe–
because my father lived his soul
love is the whole and more than all

pity this busy monster,manunkind

pity this busy monster,manunkind,

not. Progress is a comfortable disease:
your victim(death and life safely beyond)

plays with the bigness of his littleness
–electrons deify one razorblade
into a mountainrange;lenses extend

unwish through curving wherewhen till unwish
returns on its unself.
                            A world of made
is not a world of born–pity poor flesh

and trees,poor stars and stones,but never this
fine specimen of hypermagical

ultraomnipotence. We doctors know

a hopeless case if–listen:there's a hell
of a good universe next door;let's go

all which isn't singing is mere talking

all which isn't singing is mere talking
and all talking's talking to oneself
(whether that oneself be sought or seeking
master or disciple sheep or wolf)

gush to it as deity or devil
–toss in sobs and reasons threats and smiles
name it cruel fair or blessed evil–
it is you(né i)nobody else

drive dumb mankind dizzy with haranguing
–you are deafened every mother's son–
all is merely talk which isn't singing
and all talking's to oneself alone

but the very song of(as mountains
feel and lovers)singing is silence

MARK VAN DOREN   [1894–1972]

Mark Van Doren was a noted dramatist, critic, scholar, and anthologist, as well as poet. He was born in Hope, Illinois, and attended the University of Illinois, where he received his M.A. in 1915. He served in the infantry for two years during the first World War and, thereafter, spent a year in England and France on a fellowship. In 1920, he completed his Ph.D. at Columbia University, where he remained as a professor for many years. Between 1924–28, he was the literary editor for *The Nation*; from 1935–38, he was the publication's film critic.

Van Doren's *Collected Poems* was awarded the Pulitzer Prize in 1940. He produced important works of criticism on John Dryden, Edward Arlington Robinson, and William Shakespeare, and he edited the anthology *American Poets, 1630–1930*. He is best remembered for his meditative lyrics, which are reminiscent of English nature poetry.

The Distant Runners

Six great horses of Spain, set free after his death
by De Soto's men, ran West and restored to America
the wild race lost there some thousands of years ago.
—LEGEND

Ferdinand De Soto lies
Soft again in river mud.
Birds again, as on the day
Of his descending, rise and go
Straightly West, and do not know
Of feet beneath that faintly thud.

If I were there in other time,
Between the proper sky and stream;
If I were there and saw the six
Abandoned manes, and ran along,
I could sing the fetlock song
That now is chilled within a dream.

Ferdinand De Soto, sleeping
In the river, never heard
Four-and-twenty Spanish hooves
Fling off their iron and cut the green,
Leaving circles new and clean
While overhead the wing-tips whirred.

Neither I nor any walker
By the Mississippi now
Can see the dozen nostrils open
Half in pain for death of men;
But half in gladness, neighing then
As loud as loping would allow.

On they rippled, tail and back,
A prairie day, and swallows knew
A dark, uneven current there.
But not a sound came up the wind,

And toward the night their shadow thinned
Before the black that flooded through.

If I were there to bend and look,
The sky would know them as they sped
And turn to see. But I am here,
And they are far, and time is old.
Within my dream the grass is cold;
The legs are locked; the sky is dead.

Family Prime

Our golden age was then, when lamp and rug
Were one and warm, were globe against the indifferent
Million of cold things a world contains.
None there. A light shone inward, shutting out
All that was not corn yellow and love young.

Like winter bears we moved, our minds, our bodies
Jointed to fit the roundness of a room:
As sluggish, and as graceful, whether couch
Or table intercepted, or if marbles
Clicked on the floor and hunched us into play.

How long? I do not know. Before, a blank.
And after, all this oldness, them and me,
With the wind slicing in from everywhere,
And figures growing small. I may remember
Only a month of this. Or a God's hour.

Yet I remember, and my father said
He did: the moment spherical, that age
Fixes and gilds; eternity one evening
Perfect, such as maybe my own sons,
And yours, will know the taste of in their time.

And Did the Animals?

And did the animals in Noah's ark—
That was of oleander wood, with cabins
Cunningly bitumined in and out—
Did all those animals lie quietly?
For months and weeks and days, until the dove
Came home, and they were dry on Ararat,
Did every bird, with head beneath its wing,
Did every beast, with forepaws folded in,
Did every reptile, coiled upon itself,
Lie sleeping as no man did, patiently?
A man might think this tempest would not end,
Nor timbers cease to creak, nor the light come.
These did not know it rained, these did not know
Their kind survived in them if it survived.
A thinking man might doubt it, and in misery
Listen. Did they listen? But to what?
They did not know of time, they did not count
The waves. Then did they cry out in their dreams?
Or did they even dream, those specimen souls?

The Escape

Going from us at last,
He gave himself forever
Unto the mudded nest,
Unto the dog and the beaver.

Sick of the way we stood,
He pondered upon flying,
Or envied the triple thud
Of horses' hooves; whose neighing

Came to him sweeter than talk,
Whereof he too was tired.

No silences now he broke,
No emptiness explored.

Going from us, he never
Sent one syllable home.
We called him wild; but the plover
Watched him, and was tame.

CHARLES REZNIKOFF   [1894-1976]

Charles Reznikoff was born in Brooklyn, New York, the son of Russian immigrants. After a year in the School of Journalism at the University of Missouri, he enrolled in the law school of New York University; he was admitted to the bar in 1916. Reznikoff practiced law briefly and then worked as a salesman for his parents' hat company. In 1928, he took a job with a legal publishing firm and, after that, worked several years for a friend in Hollywood. Subsequently, he supported himself as a freelance writer, editor, and translator. During the thirties, he was associated with the Objectivist school of poets in New York, but it was not until New Directions brought out a selection of his work in 1962 (*By the Waters of Manhattan*) that he began to attract the attention he deserved. His poems describing the life and experiences of Jewish immigrants are particularly moving.

Five Groups of Verse, Selections

The Stars Are Hidden

The stars are hidden,
the lights are out;
the tall black houses
are ranked about.

I beat my fists
on the stout doors,
no answering steps
come down the floors.

I have walked until
I am faint and numb;
from one dark street
to another I come.

The comforting
winds are still.

This is a chaos
through which I stumble,
till I reach the void
and down I tumble.

The stars will then
be out forever;
the fists unclenched,
the feet walk never,

and all I say
blown by the wind
away.

Ghetto Funeral

Followed by his lodge, shabby men stumbling over the
     cobblestones,
and his children, faces red and ugly with tears, eyes
     and eyelids red,
in the black coffin in the black hearse the old man.

No longer secretly grieving
that his children are not strong enough to go the way
     he wanted to go
and was not strong enough.

*

Showing a torn sleeve, with stiff and shaking fingers
     the old man
pulls off a bit of the baked apple, shiny with sugar,
eating with reverence food, the great comforter.

*

She sat by the window opening into the airshaft,
and looked across the parapet
at the new moon.

She would have taken the hairpins out of her carefully
     coiled hair,
and thrown herself on the bed in tears;
but he was coming and her mouth had to be pinned
     into a smile.
If he would have her, she would marry whatever he was.

A knock. She lit the gas and opened her door.
Her aunt and the man—skin loose under his eyes,
     face slashed with wrinkles.
"Come in," she said as gently as she could and smiled.

*

Hour after hour in a rocking-chair on the porch,
hearing the wind in the shade trees.

At times a storm comes up and the dust is blown in
    long curves along the street,
over the carts driven slowly, drivers and horses nodding.

Years are thrown away as if I were immortal,
the nights spent in talking

shining words, sometimes, like fireflies in the darkness–
lighting and going out and after all no light.

A Sunny Day

The curved leaves of the little tree are shining;
the bushes across the street are purple with flowers.
A man with a red beard talks to a woman with yellow hair;
she laughs like the clash of brass cymbals.

Two Negresses are coming down the street;
they munch lettuce
and pull the leaves slowly out of a bag.

The pigeons wheel in the bright air,
now white, now the grey backs showing.
They settle down upon a roof;
the children shout, the owner swings his bamboo.

I Will Go into the Ghetto

I will go into the ghetto: the sunlight
for only an hour or two at noon
on the pavement here is enough for me;

the smell of the fields in this street
for only a day or two in spring
is enough for me.
This peace is enough for me;
let the heathen rage.

They will take away
our cakes and delicacies,
the cheerful greetings, the hours of pleasant speech, the
    smiles,
and give us back
the sight of our eyes and our silent thoughts;
they will take away our groans and sighs
and give us—
merely breath.
Breathe deeply:
how good and sweet the air is.

Let Other People Come as Streams

Let other people come as streams
that overflow a valley
and leave dead bodies, uprooted trees and fields of sand;
we Jews are as the dew,
on every blade of grass,
trodden under foot today
and here tomorrow morning.

The Body Is Like Roots Stretching Down into the Earth

The body is like roots stretching down into the earth—
forcing still a way over stones and under rock, through sand,
sucking nourishment in darkness,
bearing the tread of man and beast,
and of the earth forever;

but the spirit—
twigs and leaves
spreading
through sunshine
or the luminous darkness
of twilight, evening, night, and dawn,
moving
in every wind of heaven
and turning
to whatever corner of the sky is brightest,
compelled by nothing stronger than the light;
the body is like earth,
the spirit like water
without which earth is sand
and which must be free or stagnant;
or if the body is as water,
the spirit is like air
that must have doors and windows
or else is stuffy and unbreathable—
or like the fire
of which sun and stars have been compounded,
which Joshua could command but for an hour.

Mass Graves, Selection

About Thirty Jews Were Taken to Chelmno

About thirty Jews were taken to Chelmno
by the S.S.,
looking for strong, husky men.
At night the S.S. went around town
and grabbed people out of their beds
and took them to the headquarters of the German police.
They were then put on a truck
and S.S. men with machine guns followed them to Chelmno.
There they were put into a cellar.
On the first night, one of those in the cellar lit a little candle

and read the inscriptions on a wall:
"No one leaves this place alive"
and "When people are taken to work,
they are taken to be shot."

Next morning, when they were still in the cellar,
they heard a truckload of people arriving in the courtyard
and a voice saying:
"Now you are going to the bathhouse;
you will get new clothes and go out to work;"
and some of those in the truck began clapping their hands:
glad that they were to work–and live.
But soon those in the cellar could hear screams from the truck
as the engine began working and the gas flowed in;
and then the screams died down.

Five of the Jews were taken from the cellar
to put in a room–full of clothing and shoes–
the clothing and shoes left behind.
And the rest in the cellar
were sent to the woods
and set to digging trenches.
They would leave early in the morning
when it was still dark, for it was winter;
and when the trucks arrived
they had to wait until the fumes of the gas were gone
and then five or six would open the doors,
take out the dead
and put them right in the trenches.
One of the Jews working there
recognized a man of his own town
and remembered him as healthy and strong.
He still showed signs of life
and one of the guards shot him in the head.
Then the Ukrainians working for the Germans would come–
a Ukrainian and a German, always in pairs–
and the Ukrainians had pliers in their hands
and pulled out the gold teeth of the dead
and took off the gold rings;

and if a ring did not come off easily,
would cut off the finger.
And then there were Jews whose work it was
to place the bodies so that they formed a single layer:
a head on one side and the feet of the next body on the same side.

After the Jew who had recognized the man from his home town
had been working in the woods for some time,
other Jews from his own town were among the dead
and among them–
his wife and his two children!
He lay down next to his wife and children and wanted the Germans
    to shoot him;
but one of the S.S. men said:
"You still have enough strength to work,"
and pushed him away.
That evening he tried to hang himself
but his friends in the cellar would not let him
and said, "As long as your eyes are open,
there is hope."
The next day the man who had tried to die was on a truck.
They were still in the woods
and he asked one of the S.S. men for a cigarette.
He himself did not smoke usually
but he lit the cigarette and, when he was back where his companions
    were sitting, said:
"Look here! He gives out cigarettes.
Why don't you all ask him for a cigarette?"
They all got up–
they were in the back of the truck–
and went forwards
and he was left behind.
He had a little knife
and made a slit in the tarpaulin at the side
and jumped out;
came down on his knees
but got up and ran.
By the time the S.S. men began shooting
he was gone in the woods.

LOUISE BOGAN   [1897-1970]

Louise Bogan was born in Livermore, Maine. She was educated at Mount St. Mary's Academy in New Hampshire and the Boston Girls' Latin School, before attending Boston University for a year. *Body of This Death*, her first book of poems, appeared in 1923. Here is a finely-crafted, traditional verse, in some ways akin to that of Elinor Wylie. For many years Bogan was the poetry editor of *The New Yorker* and was known for her brief, incisive essays. In 1930, she won *Poetry* magazine's John Reed Memorial Prize and, in 1937, its Haire Levinson Prize. In her work, she evinces a fundamental insight into the problems and challenges that face women in the modern world.

Men Loved Wholly Beyond Wisdom

Men loved wholly beyond wisdom
Have the staff without the banner.
Like a fire in a dry thicket
Rising within women's eyes
Is the love men must return.
Heart, so subtle now, and trembling,
What a marvel to be wise,
To love never in this manner!
To be quiet in the fern
Like a thing gone dead and still,
Listening to the prisoned cricket
Shake its terrible, dissembling
Music in the granite hill.

Women

Women have no wilderness in them,
They are provident instead,
Content in the tight hot cell of their hearts
To eat dusty bread.

They do not see cattle cropping red winter grass,
They do not hear
Snow water going down under culverts
Shallow and clear.

They wait, when they should turn to journeys,
They stiffen, when they should bend.
They use against themselves that benevolence
To which no man is friend.

They cannot think of so many crops to a field
Or of clean wood cleft by an axe.
Their love is an eager meaninglessness
Too tense, or too lax.

They hear in every whisper that speaks to them
A shout and a cry.

As like as not, when they take life over their door-sills
They should let it go by.

Cassandra

To me, one silly task is like another.
I bare the shambling tricks of lust and pride.
This flesh will never give a child its mother,–
Song, like a wing, tears through my breast, my side,
And madness chooses out my voice again,
Again. I am the chosen no hand saves:
The shrieking heaven lifted over men,
Not the dumb earth, wherein they set their graves.

Medusa

I had come to the house, in a cave of trees,
Facing a sheer sky.
Everything moved,–a bell hung ready to strike,
Sun and reflection wheeled by.

When the bare eyes were before me
And the hissing hair,
Held up at a window, seen through a door.
The stiff bald eyes, the serpents on the forehead
Formed in the air.

This is a dead scene forever now.
Nothing will ever stir.
The end will never brighten it more than this,
Nor the rain blur.

Statue and Birds

Here, in the withered arbor, like the arrested wind,
Straight sides, carven knees,
Stands the statue, with hands flung out in alarm
Or remonstrances.

Over the lintel sway the woven bracts of the vine
In a pattern of angles.
The quill of the fountain falters, woods rake on the sky
Their brusque tangles.

The birds walk by slowly, circling the marble girl,
The golden quails,
The pheasants closed up in their arrowy wings,
Dragging their sharp tails.

The inquietudes of the sap and of the blood are spent.
What is forsaken will rest.
But her heel is lifted,–she would flee,–the whistle of the birds
Fails on her breast.

The Dream

O God, in the dream the terrible horse began
To paw at the air, and make for me with his blows.
Fear kept for thirty-five years poured through his mane,
And retribution equally old, or nearly, breathed through his nose.

Coward complete, I lay and wept on the ground
When some strong creature appeared, and leapt for the rein.
Another woman, as I lay half in a swound
Leapt in the air, and clutched at the leather and chain.

Give him, she said, something of yours as a charm.
Throw him, she said, some poor thing you alone claim.
No, no, I cried, he hates me; he's out for harm,
And whether I yield or not, it is all the same.

But, like a lion in a legend, when I flung the glove
Pulled from my sweating, my cold right hand,
The terrible beast, that no one may understand,
Came to my side, and put down his head in love.

HORACE GREGORY   [1898-1982]

Horace (Victor) Gregory was born in Milwaukee, Wisconsin and was educated at the Milwaukee School of Fine Art and the German-English Academy. Later he attended the University of Wisconsin, where he received his B.A. in 1923. It was during this time that he developed an interest in classical literature and began writing poetry. Subsequently, he moved to New York City and for several years supported himself as a free-lance writer. He married the poet Marya Zaturenska in 1925, and three years later he was awarded *Poetry* magazine's Lyric Prize. In 1934, he was appointed professor of writing at Sarah Lawrence College in Bronxville, New York, a position he held for many years. He was an active scholar and critic as well as a poet, and he published studies of Whistler and D.H. Lawrence, as well as translations of Ovid and Catullus.

They Found Him Sitting in a Chair

They found him sitting in a chair:
continual and rigid ease
poured downward through his lips and heart,
entered the lungs and spread until
paralysis possessed his knees.

The evanescent liquid still
bubbling overflows the glass
and no one heard the telephone
ringing while friends and strangers pass.
(Call taxis, wake the coroner,
police; the young ex-millionaire
is dead.) Examine unpaid bills,
insurance blanks and checks unfold
from refuse in a right-hand drawer
to read before the body's cold,

Lifelike, resembling what we were,
erect, alert the sun-tanned head:
polo or golf this afternoon?
And night, the country club or bar?

–drink down to end all poverty,
two millions gone,
                                    and stir no more.

Because I know his kind too well,
his face is mine, and the release
of energy that spent his blood
is no certificate of peace,
but like a first shot heard in war.

And not for him, nor you, nor me
that safe oblivion, that cure
to make our lives intact: immure
old debts and keep old friends.

Even in death, my lips the same
whisper at midnight through the door
and through storm-breaking hemisphere,
rise at that hour and hear my name.

Poems For My Daughter

Tell her I love
                    she will remember me
always, for she
is of my tissues made;
                         she will remember
these streets where the moon's shade
falls and my shadow mingles
with shadows sprung
from a midnight tree.
Tell her I love that I
am neither in earth nor sky,
stone nor cloud,
but only this
walled garden she knows well
and which her body is.

Her eyes alone shall make
me blossom for her sake;
contained within her, all
my days shall flower or die,
birthday or funeral
concealed where no man's eye
finds me unless she says:
He is my flesh and I
am what he was.

Ask No Return

Ask no return for love that's given
embracing mistress, wife or friend,
                              ask no return:
on this deep earth or in pale heaven,
awake and spend
hands, lips and eyes in love,
in darkness burn,
                    the limbs entwined until the soul ascend.

Ask no return of seasons gone:
the fire of autumn and the first hour of spring,
the short bough blossoming
through city windows when night's done,
when fears adjourn
                    backward in memory where all loves end
in self again, again the inward tree
growing against the heart
and no heart free.
From love that sleeps behind each eye
in double symmetry
                    ask no return,
even in enmity, look! I shall take your hand;
nor can our limbs disjoin in separate ways again,
walking, even at night on foreign land
through houses open to the wind, through cold and rain,
waking alive, meet, kiss and understand.

HART CRANE   [1899-1932]

Hart Crane was born in Garretsville, Ohio, to parents who fought frequently and ultimately divorced. His father was a candy manufacturer who hoped that Crane would pursue a business career; he was most disappointed by his son's literary inclinations. Crane left home at age seventeen, when his parents were at last divorced. He went to New York to live and work, without having finished high school. Nonetheless, he pursued his poetic endeavors and began publishing verse in journals. After spending a few years in Cleveland, working for his father, Crane returned to New York in 1923 and commenced some of his most productive, creative years. He completed the poem "Voyages" in 1924 and published his first collection, *White Buildings*, in 1926. Although Crane held jobs intermittently, his writing efforts were largely sponsored by generous friends, who often allowed him to stay in their homes, and by the gifts of the banker and patron, Otto Kahn. In 1930, Crane published *The Bridge*, which, in contrast to the pessimism of Eliot's *Waste Land*, celebrates "the Myth of America."

Crane's career as a poet spanned less than fifteen years, but during that time he established himself as an extraordinarily gifted writer, with a unique and compelling vision.

My Grandmother's Love Letters

There are no stars to-night
But those of memory.
Yet how much room for memory there is
In the loose girdle of soft rain.

There is even room enough
For the letters of my mother's mother,
Elizabeth,
That have been pressed so long
Into a corner of the roof
That they are brown and soft,
And liable to melt as snow.

Over the greatness of such space
Steps must be gentle.
It is all hung by an invisible white hair.
It trembles as birch limbs webbing the air.

And I ask myself:

"Are your fingers long enough to play
Old keys that are but echoes:
Is the silence strong enough
To carry back the music to its source
And back to you again
As though to her?"

Yet I would lead my grandmother by the hand
Through much of what she would not understand;
And so I stumble. And the rain continues on the roof
With such a sound of gently pitying laughter.

Chaplinesque

We make our meek adjustments,
Contented with such random consolations
As the wind deposits
In slithered and too ample pockets.

For we can still love the world, who find
A famished kitten on the step, and know
Recesses for it from the fury of the street
Or warm torn elbow coverts.

We will sidestep, and to the final smirk
Dally the doom of that inevitable thumb
That slowly chafes its puckered index toward us,
Facing the dull squint with what innocence
And what surprise!

And yet these fine collapses are not lies
More than the pirouettes of any pliant cane;
Our obsequies are, in a way, no enterprise.
We can evade you, and all else but the heart:
What blame to us if the heart live on.

The game enforces smirks; but we have seen
The moon in lonely alleys make
A grail of laughter of an empty ash can,
And through all sound of gaiety and quest
Have heard a kitten in the wilderness.

Possessions

Witness now this trust! the rain
That steals softly direction
And the key, ready to hand–sifting
One moment in sacrifice (the direst)
Through a thousand nights the flesh
Assaults outright for bolts that linger
Hidden,–O undirected as the sky
That through its black foam has no eyes
For this fixed stone of lust . . .

Accumulate such moments to an hour:
Account the total of this trembling tabulation.
I know the screen, the distant flying taps
And stabbing medley that sways–
And the mercy, feminine, that stays
As though prepared.

And I, entering, take up the stone
As quiet as you can make a man . . .
In Bleecker Street, still trenchant in a void,
Wounded by apprehensions out of speech,
I hold it up against a disk of light–
I, turning, turning on smoked forking spires,
The city's stubborn lives, desires.

Tossed on these horns, who bleeding dies,
Lacks all but piteous admissions to be spilt
Upon the page whose blind sum finally burns
Record of rage and partial appetites.
The pure possession, the inclusive cloud
Whose heart is fire shall come,–the white wind rase
All but bright stones wherein our smiling plays.

For the Marriage of Faustus and Helen

> *"And so we may arrive by Talmud skill*
> *And profane Greek to raise the building up*
> *Of Helen's house against the Ismaelite,*
> *King of Thogarma, and his habergeons*
> *Brimstony, blue and fiery; and the force*
> *Of King Abaddon, and the beast of Cittim;*
> *Which Rabbi David Kimchi, Onkelos,*
> *And Aben Ezra do interpret Rome."*
>
> —THE ALCHEMIST

I

The mind has shown itself at times
Too much the baked and labeled dough
Divided by accepted multitudes.
Across the stacked partitions of the day—
Across the memoranda, baseball scores,
The stenographic smiles and stock quotations
Smutty wings flash out equivocations.

The mind is brushed by sparrow wings;
Numbers, rebuffed by asphalt, crowd
The margins of the day, accent the curbs,
Convoying divers dawns on every corner
To druggist, barber and tobacconist,
Until the graduate opacities of evening
Take them away as suddenly to somewhere
Virginal perhaps, less fragmentary, cool.

> *There is the world dimensional for*
> *those untwisted by the love of things*
> *irreconcilable . . .*

And yet, suppose some evening I forgot
The fare and transfer, yet got by that way
Without recall,—lost yet poised in traffic.
Then I might find your eyes across an aisle,

Still flickering with those prefigurations—
Prodigal, yet uncontested now,
Half-riant before the jerky window frame.

There is some way, I think, to touch
Those hands of yours that count the nights
Stippled with pink and green advertisements.
And now, before its arteries turn dark
I would have you meet this bartered blood.
Imminent in his dream, none better knows
The white wafer cheek of love, or offers words
Lightly as moonlight on the eaves meets snow.

Reflective conversion of all things
At your deep blush, when ecstasies thread
The limbs and belly, when rainbows spread
Impinging on the throat and sides . . .
Inevitable, the body of the world
Weeps in inventive dust for the hiatus
That winks above it, bluet in your breasts.

The earth may glide diaphanous to death;
But if I lift my arms it is to bend
To you who turned away once, Helen, knowing
The press of troubled hands, too alternate
With steel and soil to hold you endlessly.
I meet you, therefore, in that eventual flame
You found in final chains, no captive then—
Beyond their million brittle, bloodshot eyes;
White, through white cities passed on to assume
That world which comes to each of us alone.

Accept a lone eye riveted to your plane,
Bent axle of devotion along companion ways
That beat, continuous, to hourless days—
One inconspicuous, glowing orb of praise.

II

Brazen hynotics glitter here;

Glee shifts from foot to foot,
Magnetic to their tremolo.
This crashing opéra bouffe,
Blest excursion! this ricochet
From roof to roof—
Know, Olympians, we are breathless
While nigger cupids scour the stars!

A thousand light shrugs balance us
Through snarling hails of melody.
White shadows slip across the floor
Splayed like cards from a loose hand;
Rhythmic ellipses lead into canters
Until somewhere a rooster banters.

Greet naïvely—yet intrepidly
New soothings, new amazements
That cornets introduce at every turn—
And you may fall downstairs with me
With perfect grace and equanimity.
Or, plaintively scud past shores
Where, by strange harmonic laws
All relatives, serene and cool,
Sit rocked in patent armchairs.

O, I have known metallic paradises
Where cuckoos clucked to finches
Above the deft castastrophes of drums.
While titters hailed the groans of death
Beneath gyrating awnings I have seen
The incunabula of the divine grotesque.
This music has a reassuring way.

The siren of the springs of guilty song—
Let us take her on the incandescent wax
Striated with nuances, nervosities
That we are heir to: she is still so young,
We cannot frown upon her as she smiles,
Dipping here in this cultivated storm
Among slim skaters of the gardened skies.

III

Capped arbiter of beauty in this street
That narrows darkly into motor dawn,–
You, here beside me, delicate ambassador
Of intricate slain numbers that arise
In whispers, naked of steel;
                                                      religious gunman!
Who faithfully, yourself, will fall too soon,
And in other ways than as the wind settles
On the sixteen thrifty bridges of the city:
Let us unbind our throats of fear and pity.
                                                      We even,
Who drove speediest destruction
In corymbulous formations of mechanics,–
Who hurrried the hill breezes, spouting malice
Plangent over meadows, and looked down
On rifts of torn and empty houses
Like old women with teeth unjubilant
That waited faintly, briefly and in vain:

We know, eternal gunman, our flesh remembers
The tensile boughs, the nimble blue plateaus,
The mounted, yielding cities of the air!

That saddled sky that shook down vertical
Repeated play of fire–no hypogeum
Of wave or rock was good against one hour.
We did not ask for that, but have survived,
And will persist to speak again before
All stubble streets that have not curved
To memory, or known the ominous lifted arm
That lowers down the arc of Helen's brow
To saturate with blessing and dismay.

A goose, tobacco and cologne–
Three winged and gold-shod prophecies of heaven,
The lavish heart shall always have to leaven
And spread with bells and voices, and atone
The abating shadows of our conscript dust.

Anchises' navel, dripping of the sea,—
The hands Erasmus dipped in gleaming tides,
Gathered the voltage of blown blood and vine;
Delve upward for the new and scattered wine,
O brother-thief of time, that we recall.
Laugh out the meager penance of their days
Who dare not share with us the breath released,
The substance drilled and spent beyond repair
For golden, or the shadow of gold hair.

Distinctly praise the years, whose volatile
Blamed bleeding hands extend and thresh the height
The imagination spans beyond despair,
Outpacing bargain, vocable and prayer.

At Melville's Tomb

Often beneath the wave, wide from this ledge
The dice of drowned men's bones he saw bequeath
An embassy. Their numbers as he watched,
Beat on the dusty shore and were obscured.

And wrecks passed without sound of bells,
The calyx of death's bounty giving back
A scattered chapter, livid hieroglyph,
The portent wound in corridors of shells.

Then in the circuit calm of one vast coil,
Its lashings charmed and malice reconciled,
Frosted eyes there were that lifted altars;
And silent answers crept across the stars.

Compass, quadrant and sextant contrive
No farther tides . . . High in the azure steeps
Monody shall not wake the mariner.
This fabulous shadow only the sea keeps.

The Broken Tower

The bell-rope that gathers God at dawn
Dispatches me as though I dropped down the knell
Of a spent day—to wander the cathedral lawn
From pit to crucifix, feet chill on steps from hell.

Have you not heard, have you not seen that corps
Of shadows in the tower, whose shoulders sway
Antiphonal carillons launched before
The stars are caught and hived in the sun's ray?

The bells, I say, the bells break down their tower;
And swing I know not where. Their tongues engrave
Membrane through marrow, my long-scattered score
Of broken intervals. . . . And I, their sexton slave!

Oval encyclicals in canyons heaping
The impasse high with choir. Banked voices slain!
Pagodas, campaniles with reveilles outleaping—
O terraced echoes prostrate on the plain! . . .

And so it was I entered the broken world
To trace the visionary company of love, its voice
An instant in the wind (I know not whither hurled)
But not for long to hold each desperate choice.

My word I poured. But was it cognate, scored
Of that tribunal monarch of the air
Whose thigh embronzes earth, strikes crystal Word
In wounds pledged once to hope—cleft to despair?

The steep encroachments of my blood left me
No answer (could blood hold such a lofty tower
As flings the question true?)—or is it she
Whose sweet mortality stirs latent power?—

And through whose pulse I hear, counting the strokes
My veins recall and add, revived and sure

The angelus of wars my chest evokes:
What I hold healed, original now, and pure . . .

And builds, within, a tower that is not stone
(Not stone can jacket heaven)–but slip
Of pebbles,–visible wings of silence sown
In azure circles, widening as they dip

The matrix of the heart, lift down the eye
That shrines the quiet lake and swells a tower . . .
The commodious, tall decorum of that sky
Unseals her earth, and lifts love in its shower.

Voyages

I

Above the fresh ruffles of the surf
Bright striped urchins flay each other with sand.
They have contrived a conquest for shell shucks,
And their fingers crumble fragments of baked weed
Gaily digging and scattering.

And in answer to their treble interjections
The sun beats lightning on the waves,
The waves fold thunder on the sand;
And could they hear me I would tell them:

O brilliant kids, frisk with your dog,
Fondle your shells and sticks, bleached
By time and the elements; but there is a line
You must not cross nor ever trust beyond it
Spry cordage of your bodies to caresses
Too lichen-faithful from too wide a breast.
The bottom of the sea is cruel.

II

–And yet this great wink of eternity,
Of rimless floods, unfettered leewardings,
Samite sheeted and processioned where
Her undinal vast belly moonward bends,
Laughing the wrapt inflections of our love;

Take this Sea, whose diapason knells
On scrolls of silver snowy sentences,
The sceptred terror of whose sessions rends
As her demeanors motion well or ill,
All but the pieties of lovers' hands.

And onward, as bells off San Salvador
Salute the crocus lustres of the stars,
In these poinsettia meadows of her tides,–
Adagios of islands, O my Prodigal,
Complete the dark confessions her veins spell.

Mark how her turning shoulders wind the hours,
And hasten while her penniless rich palms
Pass superscription of bent foam and wave,–
Hasten, while they are true,–sleep, death, desire,
Close round one instant in one floating flower.

Bind us in time, O Seasons clear, and awe.
O minstrel galleons of Carib fire,
Bequeath us to no earthly shore until
Is answered in the vortex of our grave
The seal's wide spindrift gaze toward paradise.

III

Infinite consanguinity it bears–
This tendered theme of you that light
Retrieves from sea plains where the sky
Resigns a breast that every wave enthrones;
While ribboned water lanes I wind

Are laved and scattered with no stroke
Wide from your side, whereto this hour
The sea lifts, also, reliquary hands.

And so, admitted through black swollen gates
That must arrest all distance otherwise,–
Past whirling pillars and lithe pediments,
Light wrestling there incessantly with light,
Star kissing star through wave on wave unto
Your body rocking!
                              and where death, if shed,
Presumes no carnage, but this single change,–
Upon the steep floor flung from dawn to dawn
The silken skilled transmemberment of song;

Permit me voyage, love, into your hands . . .

IV

Whose counted smile of hours and days, suppose
I know as spectrum of the sea and pledge
Vastly now parting gulf on gulf of wings
Whose circles bridge, I know, (from palms to the severe
Chilled albatross's white immutability)
No stream of greater love advancing now
Than, singing, this mortality alone
Through clay aflow immortally to you.

All fragrance irrefragibly, and claim
Madly meeting logically in this hour
And region that is ours to wreathe again,
Portending eyes and lips and making told
The chancel port and portion of our June–

Shall they not stem and close in our own steps
Bright staves of flowers and quills to-day as I
Must first be lost in fatal tides to tell?

In signature of the incarnate word

The harbor shoulders to resign in mingling
Mutual blood, transpiring as foreknown
And widening noon within your breast for gathering
All bright insinuations that my years have caught
For islands where must lead inviolably
Blue latitudes and levels of your eyes,–

In this expectant, still exclaim receive
The secret oar and petals of all love.

V

Meticulous, past midnight in clear rime,
Infrangible and lonely, smooth as though cast
Together in one merciless white blade–
The bay estuaries fleck the hard sky limits.

–As if too brittle or too clear to touch!
The cables of our sleep so swiftly filed,
Already hang, shred ends from remembered stars.
One frozen trackless smile . . . What words
Can strangle this deaf moonlight? For we

Are overtaken. Now no cry, no sword
Can fasten or deflect this tidal wedge,
Slow tyranny of moonlight, moonlight loved
And changed . . . "There's

Nothing like this in the world," you say,
Knowing I cannot touch your hand and look
Too, into that godless cleft of sky
Where nothing turns but dead sands flashing.

"–And never to quite understand!" No,
In all the argosy of your bright hair I dreamed
Nothing so flagless as this piracy.

                                        But now
Draw in your head, alone and too tall here.

Your eyes already in the slant of drifting foam;
Your breath sealed by the ghosts I do not know:
Draw in your head and sleep the long way home.

VI

Where icy and bright dungeons lift
Of swimmers their lost morning eyes,
And ocean rivers, churning, shift
Green borders under stranger skies,

Steadily as a shell secretes
Its beating leagues of monotone,
Or as many waters trough the sun's
Red kelson past the cape's wet stone;

O rivers mingling toward the sky
And harbor of the phoenix' breast—
My eyes pressed black against the prow,
—Thy derelict and blinded guest

Waiting, afire, what name, unspoke,
I cannot claim: let thy waves rear
More savage than the death of kings,
Some splintered garland for the seer.

Beyond siroccos harvesting
The solstice thunders, crept away,
Like a cliff swinging or a sail
Flung into April's inmost day—

Creation's blithe and petalled word
To the lounged goddess when she rose
Conceding dialogue with eyes
That smile unsearchable repose—

Still fervid covenant, Belle Isle,
—Unfolded floating dais before
Which rainbows twine continual hair—
Belle Isle, white echo of the oar!

The imaged Word, it is, that holds
Hushed willows anchored in its glow.
It is the unbetrayable reply
Whose accent no farewell can know.

The Bridge, Selection

Proem: To Brooklyn Bridge

How many dawns, chill from his rippling rest
The seagull's wings shall dip and pivot him,
Shedding white rings of tumult, building high
Over the chained bay waters Liberty–

Then, with inviolate curve, forsake our eyes
As apparitional as sails that cross
Some page of figures to be filed away;
–Till elevators drop us from our day . . .

I think of cinemas, panoramic sleights
With multitudes bent toward some flashing scene
Never disclosed, but hastened to again,
Foretold to other eyes on the same screen;

And Thee, across the harbor, silver-paced
As though the sun took step of thee, yet left
Some motion ever unspent in thy stride,–
Implicitly thy freedom staying thee!

Out of some subway scuttle, cell or loft
A bedlamite speeds to thy parapets,
Tilting there momently, shrill shirt ballooning,
A jest falls from the speechless caravan.

Down Wall, from girder into street noon leaks,
A rip-tooth of the sky's acetylene;

All afternoon the cloud-flown derricks turn . . .
Thy cables breathe the North Atlantic still.

And obscure as that heaven of the Jews,
Thy guerdon . . . Accolade thou dost bestow
Of anonymity time cannot raise:
Vibrant reprieve and pardon thou dost show.

O harp and altar, of the fury fused,
(How could mere toil align thy choiring strings!)
Terrific threshold of the prophet's pledge,
Prayer of pariah, and the lover's cry,–

Again the traffic lights that skim thy swift
Unfractioned idiom, immaculate sigh of stars,
Beading thy path–condense eternity:
And we have seen night lifted in thine arms.

Under thy shadow by the piers I waited;
Only in darkness is thy shadow clear.
The City's fiery parcels all undone,
Already snow submerges an iron year . . .

O Sleepless as the river under thee,
Vaulting the sea, the prairies' dreaming sod,
Unto us lowliest sometime sweep, descend
And of the curveship lend a myth to God.

ALLEN TATE   [1899-1979]

Allen Tate was born in Winchester, Kentucky, to a family of considerable wealth. A series of business failures made it necessary for the Tates to move often, and hence his early education was accomplished in a desultory fashion. Tate enrolled at Vanderbilt University in 1919, where he roomed with the novelist and poet Robert Penn Warren. The two so impressed their professor John Crowe Ransom that they were allowed—as undergraduates—to participate in the meetings of the Fugitives which were taking place fortnightly in Nashville. The Fugitives gathered to discuss philosophy and to critique each other's poetry; they also produced an influential journal (*The Fugitive*) in which some of Tate's verse was featured. These poems brought him to the attention of Hart Crane, and a lasting (but stormy) friendship was formed.

Tate married the novelist Caroline Gordon in 1924, and they lived for a time in Patterson, New York (with Crane as a boarder). In addition to his poetry, Tate produced biographies (*Stonewall Jackson* [1923], *Jefferson Davis* [1929]) and works of criticism. He went abroad on a Guggenheim fellowship between 1928–30 and subsequently taught at various universities. For a time, he held the Chair of Poetry at the Library of Congress. He served as editor of the *Sewanee Review* between 1944–46 and later worked for a New York publishing house. He then taught for many years at the University of Minnesota, until his retirement in his late sixties.

Mr. Pope

When Alexander Pope strolled in the city
Strict was the glint of pearl and gold sedans.
Ladies leaned out more out of fear than pity
For Pope's tight back was rather a goat's than man's.

Often one thinks the urn should have more bones
Than skeletons provide for speedy dust,
The urn gets hollow, cobwebs brittle as stones
Weave to the funeral shell a frivolous rust.

And he who dribbled couplets like a snake
Coiled to a lithe precision in the sun
Is missing. The jar is empty; you may break
It only to find that Mr. Pope is gone.

What requisitions of a verity
Prompted the wit and rage between his teeth
One cannot say. Around a crooked tree
A moral climbs whose name should be a wreath.

Mother and Son

Now all day long the man who is not dead
Hastens the dark with inattentive eyes,
The woman with white hand and erect head
Stares at the covers, leans for the son's replies
At last to her importunate womanhood–
Her hand of death laid on the living bed;
So lives the fierce compositor of blood.

She waits; he lies upon the bed of sin
Where greed, avarice, anger writhed and slept
Till to their silence they were gathered in:
There, fallen with time, his tall and bitter kin
Once fired the passions that were never kept

In the permanent heart, and there his mother lay
To bear him on the impenetrable day.

The falcon mother cannot will her hand
Up to the bed, nor break the manacle
His exile sets upon her harsh command
That he should say the time is beautiful—
Transfigured by her own possessing light:
The sick man craves the impalpable night.

Loosed betwixt eye and lid, the swimming beams
Of memory, blind school of cuttlefish,
Rise to the air, plunge to the cold streams—
Rising and plunging the half-forgotten wish
To tear his heart out in a slow disgrace
And freeze the hue of terror to her face.

Hate, misery, and fear beat off his heart
To the dry fury of the woman's mind;
The son, prone in his autumn, moves apart
A seed blown upon a returning wind.
O child, be vigilant till towards the south
On the flowered wall all the sweet afternoon,
The reaching sun, swift as the cottonmouth,
Strikes at the black crucifix on her breast
Where the cold dusk comes suddenly to rest—
Mortality will speak the victor soon!

The dreary flies, lazy and casual,
Stick to the ceiling, buzz along the wall.
O heart, the spider shuffles from the mould
Weaving, between the pinks and grapes, his pall.
The bright wallpaper, imperishably old,
Uncurls and flutters, it will never fall.

The Cross

There is a place that some men know,
I cannot see the whole of it,
Nor how men come there. Long ago
Flame burst out of a secret pit
Crushing the world with such a light
The day sky fell to moonless black,
The kingly sun to hateful night
For those, once seeing, turning back:
For love so hates mortality,
Which is the providence of life,
She will not let it blessèd be
But curses it with mortal strife.
Until beside the blinding rood
Within that world-destroying pit
–Like young wolves that have tasted blood,
Of death, men taste no more of it.
So blind, in so severe a place
(All life before in the black grave)
The last alternatives they face
Of life, without the life to save,
Being from all salvation weaned—
A stag charged both at heel and head:
Who would come back is turned a fiend
Instructed by the fiery dead.

Ode to the Confederate Dead

Row after row with strict impunity
The headstones yield their names to the element,
The wind whirrs without recollection;
In the riven troughs the splayed leaves
Pile up, of nature the casual sacrament
To the seasonal eternity of death;
Then driven by the fierce scrutiny
Of heaven to their election in the vast breath,
They sough the rumour of mortality.

Autumn is desolation in the plot
Of a thousand acres where these memories grow
From the inexhaustible bodies that are not
Dead, but feed the grass row after rich row.
Think of the autumns that have come and gone!—
Ambitious November with the humors of the year,
With a particular zeal for every slab,
Staining the uncomfortable angels that rot
On the slabs, a wing chipped here, an arm there:
The brute curiosity of an angel's stare
Turns you, like them, to stone,
Transforms the heaving air
Till plunged to a heavier world below
You shift your sea-space blindly
Heaving, turning like the blind crab.

   Dazed by the wind, only the wind
   The leaves flying, plunge

You know who have waited by the wall
The twilight certainty of an animal,
Those midnight restitutions of the blood
You know—the immitigable pines, the smoky frieze
Of the sky, the sudden call: you know the rage,
The cold pool left by the mounting flood,
Of muted Zeno and Parmenides.
You who have waited for the angry resolution
Of those desires that should be yours tomorrow,
You know the unimportant shrift of death
And praise the vision
And praise the arrogant circumstance
Of those who fall
Rank upon rank, hurried beyond decision—
Here by the sagging gate, stopped by the wall.

   Seeing, seeing only the leaves
   Flying, plunge and expire

Turn your eyes to the immoderate past,
Turn to the inscrutable infantry rising
Demons out of the earth–they will not last.
Stonewall, Stonewall, and the sunken fields of hemp,
Shiloh, Antietam, Malvern Hill, Bull Run.
Lost in that orient of the thick-and-fast
You will curse the setting sun.

   Cursing only the leaves crying
   Like an old man in a storm

You hear the shout, the crazy hemlocks point
With troubled fingers to the silence which
Smothers you, a mummy, in time.

                           The hound bitch
Toothless and dying, in a musty cellar
Hears the wind only.

                 Now that the salt of their blood
Stiffens the saltier oblivion of the sea,
Seals the malignant purity of the flood,
What shall we who count our days and bow
Our heads with a commemorial woe
In the ribboned coats of grim felicity,
What shall we say of the bones, unclean,
Whose verdurous anonymity will grow?
The ragged arms, the ragged heads and eyes
Lost in these acres of the insane green?
The gray lean spiders come, they come and go;
In a tangle of willows without light
The singular screech-owls's tight
Invisible lyric seeds the mind
With the furious murmur of their chivalry.

   We shall say only the leaves
   Flying, plunge and expire

We shall say only the leaves whispering
In the improbable mist of nightfall
That flies on multiple wing;
Night is the beginning and the end
And in between the ends of distraction
Waits mute speculation, the patient curse
That stones the eyes, or like the jaguar leaps
For his own image in a jungle pool, his victim.
What shall we say who have knowledge
Carried to the heart? Shall we take the act
To the grave? Shall we, more hopeful, set up the grave
In the house? The ravenous grave?

                                        Leave now
The shut gate and the decomposing wall:
The gentle serpent, green in the mulberry bush,
Riots with his tongue through the hush–
Sentinel of the grave who counts us all!

YVOR WINTERS   [1900-1968]

Yvor Winters was born in Chicago, Illinois. During his freshman year at the University of Chicago, he contracted tuberculosis and consequently moved to the southwest for his health. There he taught elementary and secondary school in the coal camps near Santa Fe. *The Immobile Wind*, his first book of poems, was published in 1921; it bore the influence of Pound and the Imagists. In 1925, he received an M.A. in Romance Languages from the University of Colorado and, shortly after, taught French and Spanish at the University of Idaho. He married the novelist Janet Lewis in 1927 and went to Stanford University as a teacher and graduate student. During this time, he edited *The Gyroscope* and *The Hound and the Horn*. He remained at Stanford after receiving his Ph.D. in 1934, surrounded by a group of admiring students who, in effect, constituted a distinct school of poets. Initially, Winters was better known for his sometimes caustic criticism than for his verse, though recently the poetry has come to the fore. As opposed to his early efforts, Winter's mature poetry is more traditional in tone and form. In 1961, his *Collected Poems* was awarded the Bollingen Prize.

Orpheus

In Memory of Hart Crane

Climbing from the Lethal dead,
Past the ruined waters' bed,
In the sleep his music cast
Tree and flesh and stone were fast—
As amid Dodona's wood
Wisdom never understood

Till the shade his music won
Shuddered, by a pause undone—
Silence would not let her stay.
He could go one only way:
By the river, strong with grief,
Gave his flesh beyond belief.

Yet the fingers on the lyre
Spread like an avenging fire.
Crying loud, the immortal tongue,
From the empty body wrung,
Broken in a bloody dream,
Sang unmeaning down the stream.

To a Military Rifle

The times come round again;
The private life is small;
And individual men
Are counted not at all.
Now life is general,
And the bewildered Muse,
Thinking what she has done,
Confronts the daily news.

Blunt emblem, you have won:
With carven stock unbroke,
With core of steel, with crash
Of mass, and fading smoke;
Your fire leaves little ash;
Your balance on the arm
Points whither you intend;
Your bolt is smooth with charm.
When other concepts end,
This concept, hard and pure,
Shapes every mind therefor.
The time is yours, be sure,
Old Hammerheel of War.

I cannot write your praise
When young men go to die;
Nor yet regret the ways
That ended with this hour.
The hour has come. And I,
Who alter nothing, pray
That men, surviving you,
May learn to do and say
The difficult and true,
True shape of death and power.

Sir Gawaine and the Green Knight

Reptilian green the wrinkled throat,
Green as a bough of yew the beard;
He bent his head, and so I smote;
Then for a thought my vision cleared.

The head dropped clean; he rose and walked;
He fixed his fingers in the hair;
The head was unabashed and talked;
I understood what I must dare.

His flesh, cut down, arose and grew.
He bade me wait the season's round,
And then, when he had strength anew,
To meet him on his native ground.

The year declined; and in his keep
I passed in joy a thriving yule;
And whether waking or in sleep,
I lived in riot like a fool.

He beat the woods to bring me meat.
His lady, like a forest vine,
Grew in my arms; the growth was sweet;
And yet what thoughtless force was mine!

By practice and conviction formed,
With ancient stubbornness ingrained,
Although her body clung and swarmed,
My own identity remained.

Her beauty, lithe, unholy, pure,
Took shapes that I had never known;
And had I once been insecure,
Had grafted laurel in my bone.

And then, since I had kept the trust,
Had loved the lady, yet was true,
The knight withheld his giant thrust
And let me go with what I knew.

I left the green bark and the shade,
Where growth was rapid, thick, and still;
I found a road that men had made
And rested on a drying hill.

To the Holy Spirit

from a deserted graveyard
in the Salinas Valley

Immeasurable haze:
The desert valley spreads
Up golden river-beds
As if in other days.
Trees rise and thin away,
And past the trees, the hills,
Pure line and shade of dust,
Bear witness to our wills:
We see them, for we must;
Calm in deceit, they stay.

High noon returns the mind
Upon its local fact:
Dry grass and sand; we find
No vision to distract.
Low in the summer heat,
Naming old graves, are stones
Pushed here and there, the seat
Of nothing, and the bones
Beneath are similar:
Relics of lonely men,
Brutal and aimless, then
As now, irregular.

These are thy fallen sons,
Thou whom I try to reach.
Thou whom the quick eye shuns,
Thou dost elude my speech.
Yet when I go from sense
And trace thee down in thought,
I meet thee, then, intense,
And know thee as I ought.
But thou art mind alone,
And I, alas, am bound

Pure mind to flesh and bone,
And flesh and bone to ground.

These had no thought: at most
Dark faith and blinding earth.
Where is the trammeled ghost?
Was there another birth?
Only one certainty
Beside thine unfleshed eye,
Beside the spectral tree,
Can I discern: these die.
All of this stir of age,
Though it elude my sense
Into what heritage
I know not, seems to fall,
Quiet beyond recall
Into irrelevance.

KENNETH FEARING   [1902-1961]

Kenneth Fearing was born in Oak Park, Illinois and graduated from the University of Wisconsin. He held a variety of jobs in the following years: salesman, millhand, journalist, and free-lance writer. In 1939, he taught creative writing at the League of American Writers. Fearing is often classed as one of the "proletarian poets" insofar as his rambling, witty, irreverent poems offer a radical criticism of American society. Fearing's ultimate requirement for any poem he wrote was that it be "exciting," and he prided himself on the fact that his verse discarded "the entire bag of conventions and codes usually associated with poetry." In his later years, Fearing turned to writing novels, particularly hard-boiled crime fiction.

Obituary

Take him away, he's as dead as they die,
Hear that ambulance bell, his eyes are staring straight at
    death;
Look at the fingers growing stiff, touch the face already
    cold, see the stars in the sky, look at the stains on the
    street,

Look at the ten-ton truck that came rolling along fast and
    stretched him out cold,

Then turn out his pockets and make the crowd move on.
Sergeant, what was his name? What's the driver's name?
    What's your name, sergeant?
Go through his clothes,
Take out the cigars, the money, the papers, the keys,
    take everything there is,

And give a dollar and a half to the Standard Oil. It was
    his true-blue friend.
Give the key of his flat to the D.A.R. They were friends
    of his, the best a man ever had.
Take out the pawnticket, wrap it, seal it, send it along to
    the People's Gas. They were life-long pals. It was more
    than his brother. They were just like twins.

Give away the shoes,
Give his derby away. Donate his socks to the Guggenheim
    fund,
Let the Morgans hold the priceless bills, and leaflets, and
    racing tips under lock and key,
And give Mr. Hoover the pint of gin,
Because they're all good men. And they were friends of his.

Don't forget Gene Tunney. Don't forget Will Hays. Don't
    forget Al Capone. Don't forget the I.R.T.
Give them his matches to remember him by.
They lived with him, in the same old world. And they're
    good men, too.

That's all, sergeant. There's nothing else, lieutenant.
There's no more, captain.
Pick up the body, feed it, shave it, find it another job.

Have a cigar, driver?
Take two cigars—
You were his true-blue pal.

The People vs. The People

I have never seen him, this invisible member of the panel, this thirteenth
    juror, but I have certain clues:
I know, after so many years of practice, though I cannot prove I know;
It is enough to say, I know that I know.

He is five feet nine or ten, with piercing, bright, triumphant eyes;
He needs glasses, which he will not wear, and he is almost certainly stone
    deaf.
(Cf. Blair vs. Gregg, which he utterly ruined.)
He is the juror forever looking out of the window, secretly smiling, when
    you make your telling point.
The one who is wide awake when you think he is asleep. The man who
    naps with his eyes wide open.
Those same triumphant eyes.
He is the man who knows. And knows that he knows.

His hair is meager and he wears wash ties, but these are not important
    points.
He likes the legal atmosphere, that is plain, because he is always there.
It is the decent, the orderly procedure that he likes.
He is the juror who arrived first, though you thought he was late; the one
    who failed to return from lunch, though you had not noticed.
Let me put it like this: He is the cause of your vague uneasiness when you
    glance about and see that the other twelve are all right.

I would know him if I were to see him, I could swear to his identity, if I
    actually saw him once;

I nearly overheard him, when I was for the defense: "They never indict
    anyone unless they are guilty";
And when I was the State: "A poor man (or a rich man) doesn't stand a
    chance."
Always, before the trial's end, he wants to know if the sergeant knew the
    moon was full on that particular night.

And none of this matters, except I am convinced he is the unseen juror
    bribed, bought, and planted by The People,
An enemy of reason and precedent, a friend of illogic,
Something, I now know, that I know that I really know—

And he or anyone else is welcome to my Blackstone, or my crowded
    shelves of standard books,
In exchange for the monumental works I am convinced he has been writ-
    ing through the years:
"The Rules of Hearsay"; "The Laws of Rumor";
"An Omnibus Guide to Chance and Superstition," by One Who Knows.

American Rhapsody

First you bite your fingernails. And then you comb your hair again. And
    then you wait. And wait.
(They say, you know, that first you lie. And then you steal, they say. And
    then, they say, you kill.)

Then the doorbell rings. Then Peg drops in. And Bill. And Jane. And
    Doc.
And first you talk, and smoke, and hear the news and have a drink. Then
    you walk down the stairs.
And you dine, then, and go to a show after that, perhaps, and after that a
    night spot, and after that come home again, and climb the stairs
    again, and again go to bed.

But first Peg argues, and Doc replies. First you dance the same dance and
    you drink the same drink you always drank before.
And the piano builds a roof of notes above the world.

And the trumpet weaves a dome of music through space. And the drum
    ceiling over space and time and night.
And then the table-wit. And then the check. Then home again to bed.
But first, the stairs.

And do you now, baby, as you climb the stairs, do you still feel as you did
    there?
Do you feel again as you felt this morning? And the night before? And the
    night before that?

(They say, you know, that first you hear voices. And then you have
    visions say. Then, they say, you kick and scream and rave.)

Or do you feel: What is one more night in a lifetime of nights?
What is one more death, or friendship, or divorce out of two, or three,
    Or five?
One more face among so many, many faces, one more life among so
    many lives?
But first, baby, as you climb and count the stairs (and they total the same)
    sometime or somewhere, have a different idea?
Is this, baby, what you were born to feel, and do, and be?

LANGSTON HUGHES   [1902-1967]

The foremost poet of the "Harlem Renaissance," Langston Hughes was born in Joplin, Missouri. He spent most of his early childhood in the home of his maternal grandmother, due to his parents' separation. However, he did live intermittently with each parent and each played a significant part in his intellectual development. His mother encouraged his interest in poetry; his father insisted he learn German and Spanish and funded his one year of study at Columbia University (1921-2). After this, Hughes took work on sailing vessels, travelling first to Africa and later to France. He spent time in Spain, Italy, and Paris doing odd jobs.

Returning to the United States, he moved to Washington, D.C. While working as a busboy in a hotel, he met the poet Vachel Lindsay and showed him some of his verse. Lindsay was so impressed that he included the poems in a reading at that very hotel and brought Hughes to the attention of the local literary press. Soon thereafter, Hughes was able to bring out his first volume of poems, *The Weary Blues* (1926). Supported by the White philanthropist Mrs. Amy Springarn, he enrolled in Lincoln University, where he graduated in 1929. In the following year, he published his first novel, *Not Without Laughter*, which received the Harmon Gold Award for literature. He also made several extensive reading tours in the South, which were quite successful, although some of his protest poems stirred up considerable controversy.

In addition to his literary endeavors, Hughes lent support to a variety of progressive social causes, founded Black theatres in Harlem, Chicago, and Los Angeles, and worked as a journalistic correspondent during the Spanish Civil War in 1937. In 1935, his play, *The Mulatto*, appeared on Broadway. He edited numerous Black anthologies, wrote a screenplay, and published short stories, translations, and two autobiographical volumes: *The Big Sea* (1940) and *I Wonder As I Wander* (1956). Hughes's poetry is distinguished by his use of the rhythms and cadences of jazz and the blues; it deals powerfully with racial themes and offers vivid portraits of Black life.

The Weary Blues

Droning a drowsy syncopated tune,
Rocking back and forth to a mellow croon,
    I heard a Negro play.
Down on Lenox Avenue the other night
By the pale dull pallor of an old gas light
    He did a lazy sway. . . .
    He did a lazy sway. . . .
To the tune o' those Weary Blues.
With his ebony hands on each ivory key
He made that poor piano moan with melody.
    O Blues!
Swaying to and fro on his rickety stool
He played that sad raggy tune like a musical fool.
    Sweet Blues!
Coming from a black man's soul.
    O Blues!
In a deep song voice with a melancholy tone
I heard that Negro sing, that old piano moan–
    "Ain't got nobody in all this world,
    Ain't got nobody but ma self.
    I's gwine to quit ma frownin'
    And put ma troubles on the shelf."
Thump, thump, thump, went his foot on the floor.
He played a few chords then he sang some more–
    "I got the Weary Blues
    And I can't be satisfied.
    Got the Weary Blues
    And can't be satisfied–
    I ain't happy no mo'
    And I wish that I had died."
And far into the night he crooned that tune.
    The stars went out and so did the moon.
    The singer stopped playing and went to bed
    While the Weary Blues echoed through his head.
    He slept like a rock or a man that's dead.

Homesick Blues

De railroad bridge's
A sad song in de air.
De railroad bridge's
A sad song in de air.
Ever' time de trains pass
I wants to go somewhere.

I went down to de station;
Ma heart was in ma mouth.
Went down to de station;
Heart was in ma mouth;
Lookin' for a box car
To roll me to de South.

Homesick blues, Lawd,
'S a terrible thing to have.
Homesick blues is
A terrible thing to have.
To keep from cryin'
I opens ma mouth an' laughs.

Saturday Night

Play it once.
O, play it some more.
Charlie is a gambler
An' Sadie is a whore
    A glass o' whiskey
    An' a glass o'gin:
    Strut, Mr. Charlie,
    Till de dawn comes in.
Pawn yo' gold watch
An' diamond ring.
Git a quart o' licker.
Let's shake dat thing!

Skee-de-dad! De-Dad!
Doo-doo-doo!
Won't be nothin' left
When de worms git through.
An' you's a long time
Dead
When you is
Dead, too.
So beat dat drum, boy!
Shout dat song:
Shake 'em up an' shake 'em up
All night long.
  Hey! Hey!
  Ho . . . Hum!
Do it, Mr. Charlie,
Till de red dawn come.

Jazz Band in a Parisian
Cabaret

Play that thing,
Jazz band!
Play it for the lords and ladies,
For the dukes and counts,
For the whores and gigolos,
For the American millionaires.
And the schoolteachers
Out for a spree.
Play it,
Jazz band!
You know that tune
That laughs and cries at the same time.
You know it
  May I?
  Mais oui.
  Mein Gott!
  Parece una rumba.

Play it, jazz band!
You've got seven languages to speak in
And then some,
Even if you do come from Georgia.
    Can I go home wid yuh, sweetie?
Sure.

Florida Road Workers

I'm makin' a road
For the cars
To fly by on.
Makin' a road
Through the palmetto thicket
For light and civilization
To travel on.

Makin' a road
For the rich old white men
To sweep over in their big cars
And leave me standin' here.

Sure,
A road helps all of us!
White folks ride—
And I get to see 'em ride.
I ain't never seen nobody
Ride so fine before.
Hey buddy!
Look at me.
I'm making a road!

Epilogue

I, too, sing America.

I am the darker brother.
They send me to eat in the kitchen
When company comes,
But I laugh,
And eat well,
And grow strong.

Tomorrow,
I'll sit at the table
When company comes.
Nobody'll dare
Say to me,
"Eat in the kitchen,"
Then.

Besides,
They'll see how beautiful I am
And be ashamed,–

I, too, am America.

Negro Servant

All day subdued, polite,
Kind, thoughtful to the faces that are white.
    O, tribal dance!
    O, drums!
    O, veldt at night!

Forgotten watch-fires on a hill somewhere!
O, songs that do not care!
At six o'clock, or seven, or eight,
    You're through.
    You've worked all day.
    Dark Harlem waits for you.
    The bus, the sub—
    Pay-nights a taxi
    Through the park.
O, drums of life in Harlem after dark!
    O, dreams!
    O, songs!
    O, saxophones at night!
O, sweet relief from faces that are white!

The Negro Speaks of Rivers

I've known rivers:
I've known rivers ancient as the world and
    older than the flow of human blood in
    human veins.

My soul has grown deep like the rivers.

I bathed in the Euphrates when dawns
    were young.
I built my hut near the Congo and it lulled
    me to sleep.
I looked upon the Nile and raised the
    pyramids above it.
I heard the singing of the Mississippi when
    Abe Lincoln went down to New Orleans,
    and I've seen its muddy bosom turn all
    golden in the sunset.
I've known rivers:
Ancient, dusky rivers.

My soul has grown deep like the rivers.

Cultural Exchange

In the Quarter of the Negroes
Where the doors are doors of paper
Dust of dingy atoms
Blows a scratchy sound.
Amorphous jack-o'-lanterns caper
and the wind won't wait for midnight
For fun to blow doors down.

By the river and the railroad
With fluid far-off going
Boundaries bind unbinding
A whirl of whistles blowing.
No trains or steamboats going—
Yet Leontyne's unpacking.

In the Quarter of the Negroes
Where the doorknob lets in Lieder
More than German ever bore,
Her yesterday past grandpa—
Not of her own doing—
In a pot of collard greens
Is gently stewing.

Pushcarts fold and unfold
In a supermarket sea.
And we better find out, mama,
Where is the colored laundromat
Since we moved up to Mount Vernon.

In the pot behind the paper doors
On the old iron stove what's cooking?
What's smelling, Leontyne?
Lieder, lovely Lieder
And a leaf of collard green.
Lovely Lieder, Leontyne.

You know, right at Christmas

They asked me if my blackness,
Would it rub off?
I said, *Ask your mama.*

Dreams and nightmares!
Nightmares, dreams, oh!
Dreaming that the Negroes
Of the South have taken over—
Voted all the Dixiecrats
Right out of power—
Comes the COLORED HOUR:
Martin Luther King is Governor of Georgia,
Dr. Rufus Clement his Chief Adviser,
A. Philip Randolph the High Grand Worthy.
In white pillared mansions
Sitting on their wide verandas,
Wealthy Negroes have white servants,
White sharecroppers work the black plantations,
And colored children have white mammies:
                    Mammy Faubus
                    Mammy Eastland
                    Mammy Wallace
Dear, dear darling old white mammies—
Sometimes even buried with our family.
                    Dear old
                    Mammy Faubus!
Culture, they say, *is a two-way street*:
Hand me my mint julep, mammy.
                    Hurry up!
                    Make haste!

                    Theme for English B

The instructor said,

        *Go home and write
        a page tonight.*

And let that page come out of you—
Then, it will be true.

I wonder if it's that simple?
I am twenty-two, colored, born in Winston-Salem.
I went to school there, then Durham, then here
to this college on the hill above Harlem.
I am the only colored student in my class.
The steps from the hill lead down into Harlem,
through a park, then I cross St. Nicholas,
Eighth Avenue, Seventh, and I come to the Y,
the Harlem Branch Y, where I take the elevator
up to my room, sit down, and write this page:

It's not easy to know what is true for you or me
at twenty-two, my age. But I guess I'm what
I feel and see and hear, Harlem, I hear you:
hear you, hear me—we two—you, me, talk on this page.
(I hear New York, too.) Me—who?

Well, I like to eat, sleep, drink, and be in love.
I like to work, read, learn, and understand life.
I like a pipe for a Christmas present,
or records—Bessie, bop, or Bach.
I guess being colored doesn't make me *not* like
the same things other folks like who are other races.
So will my page be colored that I write?

Being me, it will not be white.
But it will be
a part of you, instructor.
You are white—
yet a part of me, as I am a part of you.
That's American.
Sometimes perhaps you don't want to be a part of me.
Nor do I often want to be a part of you.
But we are, that's true!
As I learn from you,
I guess you learn from me—

although you're older–and white–
and somewhat more free.

This is my page for English B.

COUNTEE CULLEN   [1903–1946]

The adopted son of a Methodist minister, Countee Cullen was born and raised in New York City. After high school, he toured Europe with his father, before enrolling in New York University. There he was awarded a Witter Bynner Poetry Prize for his verse and was elected to Phi Beta Kappa upon graduating in 1925. A year later, he received his M.A. from Harvard University. He then began a life-long career as a teacher in the public schools of New York.

In 1925, his first volume of poems, *Color*, received a Harmon Gold Award. *Copper Sun* (1927) and *The Ballad of the Brown Girl* (1928) soon followed, and Cullen's reputation grew. These were the years of the Harlem Renaissance, and, indeed, Cullen was a major figure in this flowering of Black art and scholarship. For a time, he was assistant editor of *Opportunity*, a journal devoted to the development of Black writers. In 1927, Cullen brought out *Caroling Dusk*, an anthology of Black verse which stands as a landmark of the Harlem Renaissance. A Guggenheim Fellowship in 1929 helped him to complete *The Black Christ*, and, in 1932, he published *One Way to Heaven*, his only novel.

In Memory of Colonel Charles Young

Along the shore the tall, thin grass
That fringes that dark river,
While sinuously soft feet pass,
Begins to bleed and quiver.

The great dark voice breaks with a sob
Across the womb of night;
Above your grave the tom-toms throb,
And the hills are weird with light.

The great dark heart is like a well
Drained bitter by the sky,
And all the honeyed lies they tell
Come there to thirst and die.

No lie is strong enough to kill
The roots that work below;
From your rich dust and slaughtered will
A tree with tongues will grow.

Four Epitaphs

For My Grandmother

This lovely flower fell to seed;
Work gently sun and rain;
She held it as her dying creed
That she would grow again.

For John Keats, Apostle of Beauty

Not writ in water nor in mist,
Sweet lyric throat, thy name.
Thy singing lips that cold death kissed
Have seared his own with flame.

For Paul Laurence Dunbar

Born of the sorrowful of heart
Mirth was a crown upon his head;
Pride kept his twisted lips apart
In jest, to hide a heart that bled.

For a Lady I Know

She even thinks that up in heaven
    Her class lies late and snores,
While poor black cherubs rise at seven
    To do celestial chores.

Heritage

For Harold Jackman

What is Africa to me:
Copper sun or scarlet sea,
Jungle star or jungle track,
Strong bronzed men, or regal black
Women from whose loins I sprang
When the birds of Eden sang?
One three centuries removed
From the scenes his fathers loved,
Spicy grove, cinnamon tree,
What is Africa to me?

So I lie, who all day long
Want no sound except the song
Sung by wild barbaric birds
Goading massive jungle herds,
Juggernauts of flesh that pass
Trampling tall defiant grass
Where young forest lovers lie,
Plighting troth beneath the sky.

So I lie, who always hear,
Though I cram against my ear
Both my thumbs, and keep them there,
Great drums throbbing through the air.
So I lie, whose fount of pride,
Dear distress, and joy allied,
Is my somber flesh and skin,
With the dark blood dammed within
Like great pulsing tides of wine
That, I fear, must burst the fine
Channels of the chafing net
Where they surge and foam and fret.
Africa? A book one thumbs
Listlessly, till slumber comes.
Unremembered are her bats
Circling through the night, her cats
Crouching in the river reeds,
Stalking gentle flesh that feeds
By the river brink; no more
Does the bugle-throated roar
Cry that monarch claws have leapt
From the scabbards where they slept.
Silver snakes that once a year
Doff the lovely coats you wear,
Seek no covert in your fear
Lest a mortal eye should see;
What's your nakedness to me?
Here no leprous flowers rear
Fierce corollas in the air;
Here no bodies sleek and wet,
Dripping mingled rain and sweat,
Tread the savage measures of
Jungle boys and girls in love.
What is last year's snow to me,
Last year's anything? The tree
Budding yearly must forget
How its past arose or set–
Bough and blossom, flower, fruit,

Even what shy bird with mute
Wonder at her travail there,
Meekly labored in its hair.
One three centuries removed
From the scenes his fathers loved,
Spicy grove, cinnamon tree,
What is Africa to me?

So I lie, who find no peace
Night or day, no slight release
From the unremittent beat
Made by cruel padded feet
Walking through my body's street.
Up and down they go, and back,
Treading out a jungle track.
So I lie, who never quite
Safely sleep from rain at night—
I can never rest at all
When the rain begins to fall;
Like a soul gone mad with pain
I must match its weird refrain;
Ever must I twist and squirm,
Writhing like a baited worm,
While its primal measures drip
Through my body, crying, "Strip!
Doff this new exuberance.
Come and dance the Lover's Dance!"
In an old remembered way
Rain works on me night and day.

Quaint, outlandish heathen gods
Black men fashion out of rods,
Clay, and brittle bits of stone,
In a likeness like their own,
My conversion came high-priced;
I belong to Jesus Christ,
Preacher of humility;
Heathen gods are naught to me.

Father, Son, and Holy Ghost,
So I make an idle boast;
Jesus of the twice-turned cheek,
Lamb of God, although I speak
With my mouth thus, in my heart
Do I play a double part.

Ever at Thy glowing altar
Must my heart grow sick and falter,
Wishing He I served were black,
Thinking then it would not lack
Precedent of pain to guide it,
Let who would or might deride it;
Surely then this flesh would know
Yours had borne a kindred woe.
Lord, I fashion dark gods, too,
Daring even to give You
Dark despairing features where,
Crowned with dark rebellious hair,
Patience wavers just so much as
Mortal grief compels, while touches
Quick and hot, of anger, rise
To smitten cheek and weary eyes.
Lord, forgive me if my need
Sometimes shapes a human creed.

All day long and all night through,
One thing only must I do:
Quench my pride and cool my blood,
Lest I perish in the flood.
Lest a hidden ember set
Timber that I thought was wet
Burning like the dryest flax,
Melting like the merest wax,
Lest the grave restore its dead.
Not yet has my heart or head
In the least way realized
They and I are civilized.

Incident

For Eric Walrond

Once riding in old Baltimore,
  Heart-filled, head-filled with glee,
I saw a Baltimorean
  Keep looking straight at me.

Now I was eight and very small,
  And he was no whit bigger,
And so I smiled, but he poked out
  His tongue, and called me, "Nigger."

I saw the whole of Baltimore
  From May until December;
Of all the things that happened there
  That's all that I remember.

Black Majesty

After reading John W. Vandercook's
  chronicle of sable glory

These men were kings, albeit they were black,
Christophe and Dessalines and L'Ouverture;
Their majesty has made me turn my back
Upon a plaint I once shaped to endure.
These men were black, I say, but they were crowned
And purple-clad, however brief their time.
Stifle your agony; let grief be drowned;
We know joy had a day once and a clime.

Dark gutter-snipe, black sprawler-in-the-mud,
A thing men did a man may do again.
What answers filter through your sluggish blood

To these dark ghosts who knew so bright a reign?
"Lo, I am dark, but comely," Sheba sings.
"And we were black," three shades reply, "but kings."

Scottsboro, Too, Is Worth Its Song

A poem to American poets

I said:
Now will the poets sing,–
Their cries go thundering
Like blood and tears
Into the nation's ears,
Like lightning dart
Into the nation's heart.

RICHARD EBERHART   [Born 1904]

Richard Eberhart was born in Austin, Minnesota; he received a B.A. from Dartmouth College, a M.A. from St. John's College (University of Cambridge), and, in addition, did graduate work at Harvard. For a time, he was tutor to the son of the King of Siam, and, for nine years, he taught English at St. Mark's School in Massachusetts. He served as an aerial gunnery instructor in the Second World War and returned to an academic life after his discharge. For many years, he was poet-in-residence at Dartmouth. Alongside his activities as poet and professor, he found time to manage his wife's family business. Eberhart's first volume of poems appeared in 1930 (*A Bravery of Earth*); in subsequent years, he received many honors, including the Harriet Monroe and Shelley Memorial awards.

The Groundhog

In June, amid the golden fields,
I saw a groundhog lying dead.
Dead lay he; my senses shook,
And mind outshot our naked frailty.
There lowly in the vigorous summer
His form began its senseless change,
And made my senses waver dim
Seeing nature ferocious in him.
Inspecting close his maggots' might
And seething cauldron of his being,
Half with loathing, half with a strange love,
I poked him with an angry stick.
The fever arose, became a flame
And Vigour circumscribed the skies,
Immense energy in the sun,
And through my frame a sunless trembling.
My stick had done nor good nor harm.
Then stood I silent in the day
Watching the object, as before;
And kept my reverence for knowledge
Trying for control, to be still,
To quell the passion of the blood;
Until I had bent down on my knees
Praying for joy in the sight of decay.
And so I left; and I returned
In Autumn strict of eye, to see
The sap gone out of the groundhog,
But the bony sodden hulk remained.
But the year had lost its meaning,
And in intellectual chains
I lost both love and loathing,

Mured up in the wall of wisdom.
Another summer took the fields again
Massive and burning, full of life,
But when I chanced upon the spot
There was only a little hair left,

And bones bleaching in the sunlight
Beautiful as architecture;
I watched them like a geometer,
And cut a walking stick from a birch.

It has been three years now.
There is no sign of the groundhog.
I stood there in the whirling summer,
My hand capped a withered heart,
And thought of China and of Greece,
Of Alexander in his tent,
Of Montaigne in his tower,
Of Saint Theresa in her wild lament.

If I Could Only Live at the
Pitch That Is Near Madness

If I could only live at the pitch that is near madness
When everything is as it was in my childhood
Violent, vivid, and of infinite possibility:
That the sun and the moon broke over my head.

Then I cast time out of the trees and fields,
Then I stood immaculate in the Ego;
Then I eyed the world with all delight,
Reality was the perfection of my sight.

And time has big handles on the hands,
Fields and trees a way of being themselves.
I saw battalions of the race of mankind
Standing stolid, demanding a moral answer.

I gave the moral answer and I died
And into a realm of complexity came
Where nothing is possible but necessity
And the truth wailing there like a red babe.

The Fury of Aerial Bombardment

You would think the fury of aerial bombardment
Would rouse God to relent; the infinite spaces
Are still silent. He looks on shock-pried faces.
History, even, does not know what is meant.

You would feel that after so many centuries
God would give man to repent; yet he can kill
As Cain could, but with multitudinous will,
No farther advanced than in his ancient furies.

Was man made stupid to see his own stupidity?
Is God by definition indifferent, beyond us all?
Is the eternal truth man's fighting soul
Wherein the Beast ravens in its own avidity?

Of Van Wettering I speak, and Averill,
Names on a list, whose faces I do not recall
But they are gone to early death, who late in school
Distinguished the belt feed lever from the belt holding
    pawl.

Flux

The old Penobscot Indian
Sells me a pair of moccasins
That stain my feet yellow.

The gods of this world
Have taken the daughter of my neighbor,
Who died this day of encephalitis.

The absentee landlord has taken over Tree Island
Where one now hesitates to go for picnics,
Off the wide beach to see Fiddle Head.

The fogs are as unpredictable as the winds.
The next generation comes surely on,
Their nonchalance baffles my intelligence.

Some are gone for folly, some by mischance,
Cruelty broods over the inexpressible,
The inexorable is ever believable.

The boy, in his first hour on his motorbike,
Met death in a head-on collision.
His dog stood silent by the young corpse.

STANLEY KUNITZ [Born 1905]

Stanley Kunitz was born in Worcester, Massachusetts. Before his birth, his father had committed suicide when a business venture failed. While at Harvard University, Kunitz received the Garrison Prize for poetry; he graduated *summa cum laude*. In 1930, *Intellectual Things*, his first collection of poems, was published. Although it was heartily praised by other poets, by and large the book was ignored. His *Passport to the War* (1944) was consigned a similar fate, and his *Selected Poems 1928-1958* was rejected by no less than five publishers; however, in 1959 *Selected Poems* was awarded the Pulitzer Prize. Through the years, Kunitz taught at institutions such as Yale, Bennington, Columbia, and the University of Washington. In 1969, he was appointed editor of the Yale Series of Younger Poets.

The War Against the Trees

The man who sold his lawn to standard oil
Joked with his neighbors come to watch the show
While the bulldozers, drunk with gasoline,
Tested the virtue of the soil
Under the branchy sky
By overthrowing first the privet-row.

Forsythia-forays and hydrangea-raids
Were but preliminaries to a war
Against the great-grandfathers of the town,
So freshly lopped and maimed.
They struck and struck again,
And with each elm a century went down.

All day the hireling engines charged the trees,
Subverting them by hacking underground
In grub-dominions, where dark summer's mole
Rampages through his halls,
Till a northern seizure shook
Those crowns, forcing the giants to their knees.

I saw the ghosts of children at their games
Racing beyond their childhood in the shade,
And while the green world turned its death-foxed page
And a red wagon wheeled,
I watched them disappear
Into the suburbs of their grievous age.

Ripped from the craters much too big for hearts
The club-roots bared their amputated coils,
Raw gorgons matted blind, whose pocks and scars
Cried Moon! on a corner lot
One witness-moment, caught
In the rear-view mirrors of the passing cars.

The Science of the Night

I touch you in the night, whose gift was you,
My careless sprawler,
And I touch you cold, unstirring, star-
    bemused,
That are become the land of your self-
    strangeness.
What long seduction of the bone has led
    you
Down the imploring roads I cannot take
Into the arms of ghosts I never knew,
Leaving my manhood on a rumpled field
To guard you where you lie so deep
In absent-mindedness,
Caught in the calcium snows of sleep?

And even should I track you to your birth
Through all the cities of your mortal trial,
As in my jealous thought I try to do,
You would escape me—from the brink of
    earth
Take off to where the lawless auroras run,
You with your wild and metaphysic heart.
My touch is on you, who are light-years
    gone.
We are not souls but systems, and we move
In clouds of our unknowing
                          like great nebulae.
Our very motives swirl and have their start
With father lion and with mother crab.

Dreamer, my own lost rib,
Whose planetary dust is blowing
Past archipelagoes of myth and light,
What far Magellans are you mistress of
To whom you speed the pleasure of your
    art?
As through a glass that magnifies my loss

I see the lines of your spectrum shifting red,
The universe expanding, thinning out,
Our worlds flying, oh flying, fast apart.

From hooded powers and from abstract
    flight
I summon you, your person and your pride.
Fall to me now from outer space,
Still fastened desperately to my side;
Through gulfs of streaming air
Bring me the mornings of the milky ways
Down to my threshold in your drowsy eyes;
And by virtue of your honeyed word

Restore the liquid language of the moon,
That in gold mines of secrecy you delve.
Awake!
        My whirling hands stay at the noon,
Each cell within my body holds a heart
And all my hearts in unison strike twelve.

Father and Son

Now in the suburbs and the falling light
I followed him, and now down sandy road
Whiter than bone-dust, through the sweet
Curdle of fields, where the plums
Dropped with their load of ripeness, one by one.
Mile after mile I followed, with skimming feet,
After the secret master of my blood,
Him, steeped in the odor of ponds, whose indomitable love
Kept me in chains. Strode years; stretched into bird;
Raced through the sleeping country where I was young,
The silence unrolling before me as I came,
The night nailed like an orange to my brow.

How should I tell him my fable and the fears,
How bridge the chasm in a casual tone,

Saying, "The house, the stucco one you built,
We lost. Sister married and went from home,
And nothing comes back, it's strange, from where she goes.
I lived on a hill that had too many rooms:
Light we could make, but not enough of warmth,
And when the light failed, I climbed under the hill.
The papers are delivered every day;
I am alone and never shed a tear."
At the water's edge, where the smothering ferns lifted
Their arms, "Father!" I cried, "Return! You know
The way. I'll wipe the mudstains from your clothes;
No trace, I promise, will remain. Instruct
Your son, whirling between two wars,
In the Gemara of your gentleness,
For I would be a child to those who mourn
And brother to the foundlings of the field
And friend of innocence and all bright eyes.
O teach me how to work and keep me kind."
Among the turtles and the lilies he turned to me
The white ignorant hollow of his face.

A Choice of Weapons

Reviewing me without undue elation
A critic who has earned his reputation
By being always Johnny-on-the-spot
Where each contemporary starts to rot
Conceded me integrity and style
And stamina to walk a measured mile,
But wondered why a gang of personal devils
Need clank their jigging bones as public evils:

"The times are suited for the gay empiric,
The witty ironist, the casual lyric;
Apparently it's gristle-fare, not fat,
At certain tables: must we weep at that?
Though poets seem to rail at bourgeois ills

It is their lack of audience that kills.
Their metaphysics but reflects a folly:
'Read me or I'll be damned and melancholy.'
This poet suffers: that's his right, of course,
But we don't have to watch him beat his horse."

Sir, if appreciation be my lack,
You may appreciate me, front and back—
I won't deny that vaguely vulgar need:
But do not pity those whose motives bleed
Even while strolling in a formal garden.
Observe that tears are bullets when they harden;
The triggered poem's no water-pistol toy,
But shoots its cause, and is a source of joy.

ROBERT PENN WARREN [Born 1905]

Robert Penn Warren was born in Guthrie, Kentucky, and educated at Vanderbilt University. Originally, he had intended to major in the sciences, but he found freshman English so engaging that he decided instead to study literature. While at Vanderbilt he met Allen Tate who introduced him to the Fugitives, the poetry and philosophy society organized by John Crowe Ransom. In subsequent years, Warren furthered his studies at Yale and at Oxford, on a Rhodes Scholarship. He taught at various colleges across the country before joining the Yale faculty in 1950. Warren is noted for his novels and his insightful criticism, as well as for his verse. His novel *All the King's Men* (1946) was awarded a Pulitzer Prize, as was a collection of verse, *Promises*, in 1958. Furthermore, *Understanding Poetry*, a textbook he wrote with Cleanth Brooks, became a classic of its kind and exerted a profound influence on the manner in which literature was taught in American colleges.

Pondy Woods

The buzzards over Pondy Woods
Achieve the blue tense altitudes,
Black figments that the woods release,
Obscenity in form and grace,
Drifting high through the pure sunshine
Till the sun in gold decline.

Big Jim Todd was a slick blackbuck
Laying low in the mud and muck
Of Pondy Woods when the sun went down
In gold, and the buzzards tilted down
A windless vortex to the black-gum trees
To sit along the quiet boughs,
Devout and swollen, at their ease.

By the buzzard roost Big Jim Todd
Listened for hoofs on the corduroy road
Or for the foul and sucking sound
A man's foot makes on the marshy ground.
Past midnight, when the moccasin
Slipped from the log and, trailing in
Its obscured waters, broke
The dark algae, one lean bird spoke.

"Nigger, you went this afternoon
For your Saturday spree at the Blue Goose saloon,
So you've got on your Sunday clothes,
On your big splay feet got patent-leather shoes.
But a buzzard can smell the thing you've done;
The posse will get you—run, nigger, run—
There's a fellow behind you with a big shot-gun.

Nigger, nigger, you'll sweat cold sweat
In your patent-leather shoes and Sunday clothes
When down your track the steeljacket goes
Mean and whimpering over the wheat.

"Nigger, your breed ain't metaphysical."
The buzzard coughed. His words fell
In the darkness, mystic and ambrosial.
"But we maintain our ancient rite,
Eat gods by day and prophesy by night.
We swing against the sky and wait;
You seize the hour, more passionate
Than strong, and strive with time to die—
With Time, the beaked tribe's astute ally.

"The Jew-boy died. The Syrian vulture swung
Remotely above the cross whereon he hung
From dinner-time to supper-time, and all
The people gathered there watched him until
The lean brown chest no longer stirred,
Then idly watched the slow majestic bird
That in the last sun above the twilit hill
Gleamed for a moment at the height and slid
Down the hot wind and in the darkness hid:
Nigger, regard the circumstance of breath:
'Non omnis moriar,' the poet saith."

Pedantic, the bird clacked its gray beak,
With a Tennessee accent to the classic phrase;
Jim understood, and was about to speak,
But the buzzard drooped one wing and filmed the eyes.

At dawn unto the Sabbath wheat he came,
That gave to the dew its faithless yellow flame
From kindly loam in recollection of
The fires that in the brutal rock once strove.
To the ripe wheat fields he came at dawn.
Northward the printed smoke stood quiet above
The distant cabins of Squiggtown.
A train's far whistle blew and drifted away
Coldly; lucid and thin the morning lay
Along the farms, and here no sound
Touched the sweet earth miraculously stilled.
Then down the damp and sudden wood there belled
The musical white-throated hound.

In Pondy Woods in the August drouth
Lurks fever and the cottonmouth.
And buzzards over Pondy Woods
Achieve the blue tense altitudes,

Drifting high in the pure sunshine
Till the sun in gold decline;
Then golden and hieratic through
The night their eyes burn two by two.

Bearded Oaks

The oaks, how subtle and marine,
Bearded, and all the layered light
Above them swims; and thus the scene,
Recessed, awaits the positive night.

So, waiting, we in the grass now lie
Beneath the languorous tread of light:
The grasses, kelp-like, satisfy
The nameless motions of the air.

Upon the floor of light, and time,
Unmurmuring, of polyp made,
We rest; we are, as light withdraws,
Twin atolls on a shelf of shade.

Ages to our construction went,
Dim architecture, hour by hour:
And violence, forgot now, lent
The present stillness all its power.

The storm of noon above us rolled,
Of light the fury, furious gold,
The long drag troubling us, the depth:
Dark is unrocking, unrippling, still.

Passion and slaughter, ruth, decay
Descend, minutely whispering down,
Silted down swaying streams, to lay
Foundation for our voicelessness.

All our debate is voiceless here,
As all our rage, the rage of stone;
If hope is hopeless, then fearless is fear,
And history is thus undone.

Our feet once wrought the hollow street
With echo when the lamps were dead
At windows, once our headlight glare
Disturbed the doe that, leaping, fled.

I do not love you less that now
The caged heart makes iron stroke,
Or less that all that light once gave
The graduate dark should now revoke.

We live in time so little time
And we learn all so painfully,
That we may spare this hour's term
To practice for eternity.

Debate: Question, Quarry, Dream

Asking what, asking what?–all a boy's afternoon,
Squatting in the canebrake where the muskrat will come.
Muskrat, muskrat, please now, please, come soon.
He comes, stares, goes, lets the question resume.
He has taken whatever answer may be down to his mud-
    burrow gloom.

Seeking what, seeking what?–foot soft in cedar-shade.
Was that a deer-flag white past windfall and fern?
No, but by bluffside lurk powers and in the fern-glade

Tall presences, standing all night, like white fox-fire burn.
The small fox lays his head in your hand now and weeps
  that you go, not to return.

Dreaming what, dreaming what?–lying on the hill at
  twilight,
The still air stirred only by moth wing, and the last stain
  of sun

Fading to moth-sky, blood-red to moth-white and starlight,
And Time leans down to kiss the heart's ambition,
While far away, before moonrise, come the town lights,
  one by one.

Long since that time I have walked night streets, heel-iron
Clicking the stone, and in dark in windows have stared.
Question, quarry, dream–I have vented my ire on
My own heart that, ignorant and untoward,
Yearns for an absolute that Time would, I thought, have
  prepared,

But has not yet. Well, let us debate
The issue. But under a tight roof, clutching a toy,
My son now sleeps, and when the hour grows late,
I shall go forth where the cold constellations deploy
And lift up my eyes to consider more strictly the ap-
  palling logic of joy.

INDEX

Poet names are in bold face; poem titles are in italics; and poem first lines are enclosed in quotation marks.

ACKNOWLEDGMENTS

Permission to reprint copyrighted poems is
gratefully acknowledged to the following:

ALFRED A. KNOPF, INC., for "Sunday Morning;" "Disillusionment of Ten O'Clock;" "Thirteen Ways of Looking at a Blackbird;" "Metaphors of a Magnifico;" "Anecdote of the Jar;" "A High-Toned Old Christian Woman;" "The Emperor of Ice-Cream;" from *The Collected Poems of Wallace Stevens.* Copyright 1923 & copyright renewed 1951 by Wallace Stevens. "The Idea of Order at Key West;" "Evening Without Angels;" from *The Collected Poems of Wallace Stevens.* Copyright 1936 by Wallace Stevens. Copyright renewed 1964 by Holly Stevens. "The Ultimate Poem Is Abstract;" "Dutch Graves in Bucks County;" from *The Collected Poems of Wallace Stevens.* Copyright 1942 by Wallace Stevens. "Of Modern Poetry;" from *The Collected Poems of Wallace Stevens.* Copyright 1942 by Wallace Stevens. Copyright renewed 1970 by Holly Stevens. "Of Mere Being;" "As You Leave the Room;" "The Sail of Ulysses;" from *Opus Posthumous* by Wallace Stevens. Copyright 1957 by Elsie Stevens and Holly Stevens. "Dead Boy;" "Piazza Piece;" "Two in August;" "Janet Waking;" "Antique Harvesters;" "Blue Girls;" "Dog;" "The Equilibrists;" from *Selected Poems, Third Edition, Revised and Enlarged* by John Crowe Ransom. Copyright 1927 by Alfred A. Knopf, Inc.. Copyright renewed 1955 by John Crowe Ransom. "Bells for John Whiteside's Daughter;" "Captain Carpenter;" "Here Lies a Lady;" from *Selected Poems, Third Edition, Revised and Enlarged* by John Crowe Ransom. Copyright 1934 by Alfred A. Knopf, Inc.. Copyright renewed 1952 by John Crowe Ransom. "Painted Head;" from *Selected Poems, Third Edition, Revised and Enlarged* by John Crowe Ransom. Copyright 1934 by Alfred A. Knopf, Inc.. Copyright renewed 1962 by John Crowe Ransom. "The Negro Speaks of Rivers;" "I, Too" (Epilogue); "The Weary Blues;" from *Selected Poems of Langston Hughes.* Copyright 1926 by Alfred A. Knopf, Inc.. Copyright renewed 1954 by Langston Hughes. "Cultural Exchange;" from *The Panther and the Lash* by Langston Hughes. Copyright 1961 by Langston Hughes. "Florida Road Workers;" from *Selected Poems of Langston Hughes.* Copyright 1967 by Langston Hughes. "Homesick Blues;" from *The Dream Keeper and Other Poems* by Langston Hughes. Copyright 1927 by Alfred A. Knopf, Inc.. Copyright renewed 1955 by Langston Hughes.
BLACK SPARROW PRESS, for "The Stars Are Hidden;" "Ghetto Funeral;" "A Sunny Day;" "I Will Go into the Ghetto;" "Let Other People Come as Streams;" "The Body Is Like Roots Stretching Down into the Earth" and "About Thirty Jews Were Taken to Chelmo" by Charles Reznikoff. Copyright © by Charles Reznikoff.
CHARLES SCRIBNER'S SONS, for "Always, From My First Boyhood" and "In the Dordogne" from *The Collected Poems of John Peale Bishop* by Allen Tate. Copyright 1948 by Charles Scribner's Sons. Copyright renewed 1976 by Charles Scribner's Sons.
FARRAR, STRAUS & GIROUX, INC., for "Men Loved Wholly Beyond Wisdom;" "Women;" "Cassandra;" "Medusa;" "Statue and Birds;" "The Dream" from *The Blue Estuaries* by Louise Bogan. Copyright 1923, 1933, 1941, 1957, 1962, 1968 by Louise Bogan. "Mr. Pope;" "Mother and Son;" "The Cross;" "Ode to the Confederate Dead" from *Collected Poems 1919–1976* by Allan Tate. Copyright 1952, 1953, 1970, 1977 by Allan Tate. Copyright 1931, 1932, 1937, 1948 by Charles Scribner's Sons. Copyright renewed 1959, 1960, 1965 by Allan Tate. "The Distant Runners;" "Family Prime;" "And Did the Animals" and "The Escape" from *Collected and New Poems 1924–1963* by Mark Van Doren. Copyright 1963 by Mark Van Doren.
HARCOURT BRACE JOVANOVICH, INC., for "anyone lived in a pretty how town" and "my father moved through dooms of love". Reprinted from *Complete Poems 1913-1962.* Copyright 1940 by E.E. Cummings; renewed 1968 by Marion Morehouse Cummings. "pity this busy monster, manunkind" reprinted from *Complete Poems 1913-1962* by E.E. Cummings. Copyright 1944 by E.E. Cummings; renewed 1972 by Nancy T. Andrews. "all which isn't singing is mere talking" reprinted from *Complete Poems 1913-1962.* Copyright 1963 by Marion Morehouse Cummings. "The Love Song of J. Alfred Prufrock;" "Rhapsody on a Windy Night;" "The Waste Land" and "The Hollow Men" from *Collected Poems 1909–1962* by T.S. Eliot. Copyright 1936 by Harcourt Brace Jovanovich, Inc.; copyright © 1963, 1964 by T.S. Eliot. "Burnt Norton" in *Four Quartets* by T.S. Eliot. Copyright 1943 by T.S. Eliot; renewed 1971 by Esme Valerie Eliot.

HAROLD OBER ASSOCIATES INCORPORATED, for "Saturday Night" and "Jazz Band in a Parisian Cabaret;" Copyright 1927 by Alfred A. Knopf Inc. Copyright renewed 1955 by Langston Hughes. "Negro Servant;" Copyright 1948 by Alfred A. Knopf, Inc. "Theme for English B;" Copyright 1951 by Langston Hughes. Copyright renewed 1979 by George Houston Bass.

HARPER & ROW, PUBLISHERS, INC., for "Incident;" "Heritage;" "Epitaphs" (four). Copyright 1925 by Harper & Row, Publishers, Inc. Renewed 1953 by Ida M. Cullen. "Black Majesty". Copyright 1929 by Harper & Row, Publishers, Inc. Renewed 1957 by Ida M. Cullen. "Scottsboro, Too, Is Worth a Song". Copyright 1935 by Harper & Row, Publishers, Inc. Renewed 1963 by Ida M. Cullen. From *On These I Stand* by Countee Cullen. "In Memory of Colonel Charles Young" from *Color* by Countee Cullen. Copyright 1925 by Harper & Row, Publishers, Inc. Renewed 1953 by Ida M. Cullen.

HOUGHTON MIFFLIN COMPANY, for "Memorial Rain;" "Ars Poetica;" "You, Andrew Marvell;" "The End of the World;" "Epistle to Be Left in the Earth;" "The Speech to a Crown;" "Immortal Autumn;" "Tourist Death;" "Invocation to the Social Muse" from *New and Collected Poems 1917-1976* by Archibald MacLeish. Copyright 1976 by Archibald MacLeish. "The Reconciliation" from *The Human Season* by Archibald MacLeish. Copyright 1972 by Archibald MacLeish.

JEFFERS LITERARY PROPERTIES, for "Age in Prospect" and "Clouds of Evening" by Robinson Jeffers.

LITTLE, BROWN AND COMPANY, in association with THE ATLANTIC MONTHLY PRESS, for "The War Against the Trees;" "The Science of the Night;" "Father and Son;" "A Choice of Weapons" from *The Poems of Stanley Kunitz 1928-1978* by Stanley Kunitz. Copyright 1944, 1955, 1956, 1957 by Stanley Kunitz.

LIVERIGHT PUBLISHING CORPORATION, for "My Grandmother's Love Letters;" "Chaplinesque;" "Possessions;" "For the Marriage of Faustus and Helen;" "Voyages;" "At Melville's Tomb;" from *The Bridge* "Proem: To Brooklyn Bridge;" "The Broken Tower" from *The Complete Poems And Selected Letters And Prose Of Hart Crane*, Edited by Brom Weber. Copyright 1933, © 1958, 1966 by Liveright Publishing Corporation.

MACMILLAN PUBLISHING COMPANY, for "No Swan So Fine;" "The Fish;" "In This Age of Hard Trying;" "Critics and Connoisseurs;" "The Monkeys;" "England;" "Poetry;" "A Grave;" "The Pangolin;" "Spenser's Ireland;" "What Are Years?" "In Distrust of Merits" from *Collected Poems* by Marianne Moore. Copyright 1935 by Marianne Moore, renewed 1963 by Marianne Moore and T.S. Eliot. Copyright 1941, 1944, band renewed 1969, 1972 by Marianne Moore.

NEW DIRECTIONS PUBLISHING CORPORATION, for "Orpheus;" "To a Military Rifle;" "Sir Gawaine and the Green Knight" from *Collected Poems* by Yvor Winters. Copyright 1943 by New Directions Publishing Corporation.

OHIO UNIVERSITY PRESS, for "To the Holy Spirit" from *The Collected Poems of Ivor Winters*, 1978, Swallow Press.

OXFORD UNIVERSITY PRESS, INC., for "The Groundhog;" "If I Could Only Live . . . ;" "The Fury of Aerial Bombardment;" "Flux" from *Collected Poems 1930-1976* by Richard Eberhart. Copyright 1960, 1976 by Richard Eberhart.

RANDOM HOUSE, INC., for "Pondy Woods;" from *Selected Poems 1923-1975* by Robert Penn Warren. Copyright 1944 by Robert Penn Warren. "Bearded Oaks;" from *Selected Poems 1923-1975* by Robert Penn Warren. Copyright 1942 & copyright renewed 1970 by Robert Penn Warren. "Debate: Question, Quarry, Dream;" from *Selected Poems 1923-1975* by Robert Penn Warren. Copyright 1958 by Robert Penn Warren. "Post Mortem;" "Ante Mortem;" "Night;" "Apology for Bad Dreams;" "Shine, Perishing Republic;" from *The Selected Poetry of Robinson Jeffers*. Copyright 1925 & copyright renewed 1953 by Robinson Jeffers. "Hurt Hawks;" 1928 & copyright renewed 1956 by Robinson Jeffers. "New Mexican Mountain;" from *The Selected Poetry of Robinson Jeffers*. Copyright 1932 & copyright renewed 1960 by Robinson Jeffers. "Ave Caesar;" from *The Selected Poetry of Robinson Jeffers*. Copyright 1935 & copyright renewed 1963 by Donnan Jeffers and Garth Jeffers.

RUSSELL VOLKENING, INC., as agents for the author, for "Obituary" and "American Rhapsody" from *New and Selected Poems* by Kenneth Fearing. Copyright 1956, renewed 1984. "The People Vs. The People" originally published in *The New Yorker*, March 6, 1948. Copyright 1956, renewed 1984.